CRICUT MAKER SERIES 2

This Book Includes : "Cricut for Beginners + Cricut Design Space + Cricut Maker Machine"

By Noemi Maker and Melissa Johnson

CRICUT SERIES

Cricut for Beginners

Cricut Design Space

Cricut Maker Machine

Cricut for Beginners

The Beginners Guide to Master your Cricut Maker with many Ideas, Projects, and much more..

By Noemi Maker

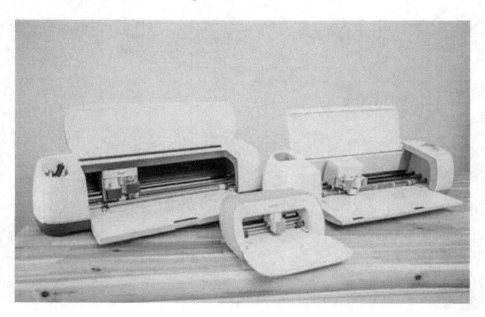

The information herein is offered for informational purposes solely, and is universal as so. The presentation of the information is without contract or any type of guarantee assurance.

The trademarks that are used are without any consent, and the publication of the trademark is without permission or backing by the trademark owner. All trademarks and brands within this book are for clarifying purposes only and are the owned by the owners themselves, not affiliated with this document.

Introduction

This book is about the Cricut Maker. It is the latest die- cutting machine from Cricut. If you have recently bought a Cricut Maker or are planning to buy one, this book is for you. Out of the entire Cricut range of machines, the Cricut Maker is the most advanced. It cuts and shapes more than 300 different kinds of materials. The Cricut Maker can be termed as the flagship machine of Cricut. It has been announced that any more blades or tips that will be introduced in the future by the company will be compatible with the Cricut Maker.

Cricut Maker is an extraordinary machine. It can cut, deboss, score, engrave, foil, perforate a large variety of materials. The best thing about it is that it can cut through lightweight materials like crepe paper to the much heavier materials like wood sheets and chipboard. This versatility sets it apart from all the other machines in the Cricut Family. The possibilities are unlimited.

The Cricut Maker is operated by a software known as the Design Space. All creativity and design are done through this program. This software is used for all the Cricut machines. It is an extremely user-friendly program. However, it might be a bit hard for a first time Cricut user. A detailed explanation of the usage is provided in the book. You can create your designs and start with some already installed projects that come free with Cricut Maker. You can also join Cricut Access, a subscription service from Cricut, where you can access hundreds of pre-made projects and fonts. You also have an option to upload and share your work with the Cricut community.

There are endless opportunities with your Cricut Maker. You can use it for your home projects such as cards, gift boxes, stencils, customized mugs, t-shirts, etc. You can also start your own business by selling your crafts and making customized merchandise for parties and events. You can also earn money by giving tutorials of your DIY Cricut crafts. It is a horizon of possibilities.

Chapter 1. The Cricut Maker

(The Cricut Maker)

The Cricut Maker is the most evolved of the Cricut family. It is the most powerful machine till now. With the Cricut Maker, you have so many possibilities at your fingertips. It will take your creative potential to a whole new level. The functions are not limited to cutting only. It can engrave, emboss, score, and foil as well. All these functions are explained in the following chapters. First, we will start with the exceptional qualities and features of this extraordinary machine:

- It can cut and shape up to 300+ different materials. This capability sets it ahead of every other machine available.
- The project size it can create usually is 12inches by 12inches. The maximum size it can create is 12inches by 24inches in length.
- The Cricut Maker is perfect for professional-level DIY projects because of its ability to cut various materials, precision, and accuracy.
- The Design Space software it uses is compatible with iOS, Mac, Android, and Windows.
- It can be connected to the computer or other device with a USB port as well as Bluetooth.
- It can be effectively used for small businesses due to its commercial-grade performance.
- It has more than ten blades and tips for various functions.
- The Cricut Maker cuts with a pressure of 4kg. It is ten times more than any other machine. Not only does it cut with this pressure, but it has a built-in sensor to guide it to cut with adequate pressure according to the material with brilliant precision.
- The Cricut Maker has a new feature of the adaptive tool system. This means that it is compatible and will fit with all the available Cricut tools. It will be compatible with all the new tools to be released by Cricut in the future. Thus the need for upgrading your Cricut machine will not be required.
- The Cricut Maker has a unique rotary tool that is used for cutting all kinds of fabric. This is a new blade and is exclusive to the Cricut Maker.

- If you are working with a smartphone or a tablet, the Cricut Maker has a docking slot for them to be placed. This helps a lot while designing the projects.
- With the Cricut Machine purchase, you get access to fifty pre-programmed projects, including twenty-five sewing projects.
- With the purchase of a Cricut Maker, you get a free trial period for Cricut Access.

With all these features, your imagination can become a reality with just a little effort. For the first time buyer of the Cricut Maker, the blades and equipment can be intimidating. The thought of understanding and running a whole new software can also be a scare for some. But do not you worry. We have all of that covered.

In our following chapter, we will discuss all the Cricut Maker hardware and features, and in the next chapter, we will explain the Design Space software in depth.

Unboxing of the Cricut Maker

We have entered the most exciting part of our book. The unboxing of the Cricut Maker. Currently, the Cricut Maker is available in five different colors:

1. Lilac
2. Blue
3. Rose
4. Mint
5. Champagne

The Cricut Maker is sold stand-alone and with an Essential bundle option and the Everything Bundle option. The Essential Bundle includes some stuff to start a new project. These might be Cricut types of vinyl, Cricut textured paper, and Cricut cardstock. Similarly, the Everything Bundle also includes helpful materials to start away new projects immediately. Here we will discuss all the standard Cricut Maker and what comes with a basic Cricut Maker. When you open your Cricut Maker, you will find the following stuff:

- Cricut Maker machine
- Instruction Booklet
- One black fine tip pen
- 50 free projects in Design Space for practice
- Materials for a practice project
- Power adapter
- USB cable
- Light Grip Machine Mat (Standard Size)
- Pink Colored Fabric Grip Mat (Standard Size)
- Rotary Blade with housing
- Fine point blade with housing
- Trial membership for Design Access (Free)

Sometimes the fine point blade with the housing is already installed in the Cricut Maker. So, do not worry if you cannot find it right away. First, check inside the Cricut Maker. Most probably, the blade is already installed.

Cricut Blades

As mentioned earlier, the Cricut maker can cut more than 300 materials. But since each material has different characteristics, so the blades for their cutting are also different. The Cricut Maker is the most advanced in the Cricut Machines. It has the greatest number of blades compatible with its hardware. The best thing about the Cricut Maker is that in the future, when Cricut makes any more blades, they are all going to be compatible with the Cricut Maker. So, to invest in the Cricut maker should prove to be a sagacious decision. This chapter will discuss all the blades compatible with the Cricut Maker, their specific housing, and their usage.

(Cricut Blades and Tips)

- Fine Point Blade

The housing for this blade is either golden or silver. The fine point blade is used to cut light to medium weight materials. Some materials that can be cut using the fine point blade are:

- Crepe paper
- Simple paper
- Textured paper
- Cardstock
- Iron on viny

If you are a beginner, this blade is just for you.

- Deep Cut Blade

This blade has black housing. This blade cuts deeper than the fine point blade. The materials that can be used to cut with this blade are medium-weight materials. Following materials are advised to be cut using the deep cut blade:

- Thick cardstock

- Magnetic strips
- Chipboard
- Foam sheets
- Soft leather

This is also a handy blade for slightly more detailed projects.

- Bonded Fabric Blade

This blade has a pink housing. As the name specifies, this blade is a fabric only band. This can be used to cut:

- Bonded fabrics
- Fabric with and iron on the backs

This blade is compatible with the Cricut Explorer machine as well.

Blades Exclusive to the Cricut Maker

The Cricut Maker is the most advanced of the Cricut familu and it has the most number of blades and cutting tools. Along with cutting the Cricut Maker has a number of speciality blades and tips for functions other than cutting. It has more than eleven functional blades and tips. Also, the best thing is that Cricut has announced that if it launches any more speciality tools or blades, the will be compatible with the cricut maker. So if you have a cricut maker, you do not need to worry about changing your machine any time soon.

Here is a detailed explanation of all the blades and speciality tips of the cricut maker:

- Rotary Blade

Now, this blade is a significant feature of the Cricut Maker. This rotary blade is exclusive to the Cricut Maker. This blade has a silver housing. The specialty of this blade is that it will cut through any fabric. Apart from the fabric, it can cut cork and tissue paper.

- Knife Blade

This blade is exclusive to the Cricut Maker. It is not a part of the blades provided with the Cricut Maker. S, you must buy this separately. This blade is used to cut through much thicker material. Such as:

- Thick leather
- Chipboard
- Think wood
- Magnetic strip

This feature can be helpful with a lot of materials that cannot be cut with regular scissors.

Specialty tools For Cricut Maker

Apart from all the blades, there are some special tools for other functions other than only cutting.

- Pens and Markers

With the slots for the blade housings, there is a slot for pens and markers. This is used if you want to make greeting cards and want beautiful fonts. There is a variety of pens and markers compatible with the Cricut. You must buy Markers and Pens separately.

- Quick Swap Housing and Tips

This is a single housing, and several function tips can be used with the same housing. Following is an explanation regarding the tips that can be used interchangeably with this housing.

❖ Scoring Wheel

This is a unique feature. If you do not need to cut in a design but fold a piece of material, this scoring wheel is your friend. The uses for this feature are:

- Making custom boxes
- Making greeting cards

There are two types of scoring tips, single and double. You can use the same housing for both types of tips, depending on your project.

❖ Foil Transfer Tip

This one is one of the latest features of the Cricut Maker. This is used to decorate and add bling to the creations. It is used with foil sheets.

❖ Engrave tip

This tip can be used to engrave different materials with either texts or monograms. It works better on sturdy materials such as plastic sheets, metal sheets, and leather. You can personalize your designs with this tip.

❖ Deboss tip

This one is like the engraving tip but is more specific for softer and lighter materials. It can be used to decorate foil, thick card stock, and basswood.

❖ Perforation Tip

Sometimes a project requires tear-off materials. for this purpose, the perforation tip is used. This tip is more compatible with lightweight materials

❖ Wavy tip

This tip is handy for making greeting cards. This gives wavy edges, which give a decorative finish. It can be used to design the edges of cards, can be used for iron-on vinyl and other textured papers.

Cricut Grip Mats

(Cricut Grip Mats)

Cricut maker comes with Grip Machine mats. When you buy a Cricut Maker, it comes with one Standard Fabric Grip Machine Mat and the other Standard Light Grip Machine Mat. So, what exactly are the grip mats? Mats provide the surface for the material to be cut. The choice of mats depends upon the material you are working with. There is a different mat for different materials. Cricut has four different types of mats.

- Fabric Grip Machine Mat
- Light Grip Machine Mat
- Standard Grip Machine Mat
- Strong Grip Machine Mat

Each mat has a different color. All the mats have a protective cover of a transparent sheet to save the mat from dirt and dust. The out rim of all the mats is smooth, and the whole of the inner part has a sticky surface. The sticky surface is for the easy adherence of the cutting materials to the mat. The stickiness depends on the materials being cut. All the mats are calibrated into 1-inch squares. The centimeter measurements are also given at the bottom and right sides of the mats. Each of these mats is available in two sizes. The standard size is 12 by 12 inches, and the larger one is 12 by 24 inches for bigger projects. The importance of the mats lies in the fact that you will require these mats for all the projects. All materials require a surface to be placed and loaded into the machine. The mats provide this surface. Here is a detailed explanation of the functionality of each mat.

Fabric Grip Machine Mat:

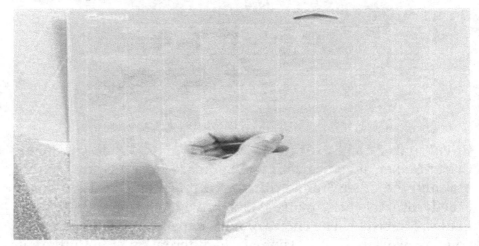

(Cricut Fabric Grip Mat)

As the name suggests, this mat is for fabrics. The fabric mats are pink in color. It has adequate stickiness for all types of fabrics. When you use the rotary blade for the cutting of fabric, this mat is required. The mat catches dust quite easily, so it needs a lot of care.

Light Grip Machine mat:

(Cricut Light Grip Mat)

This mat is blue. This has the least amount of stickiness. So, this one is used for lightweight materials. The materials suitable for this mat are:

- Simple paper
- Regular vinyl
- Thin cardstock
- Crape Paper

Standard Grip Machine Mat:

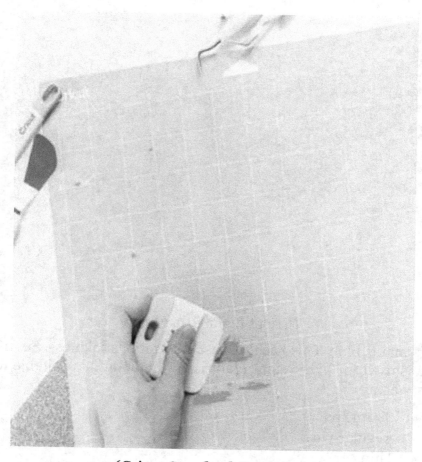

(Cricut Standard Grip Mat)

This mat is green in color. This mat can be used for almost all the materials you might want to cut. You might use this mat for most of your projects. It can adhere to materials more than the light grip mat. The materials that can be cut with it are:

- Simple cardstock
- Removable vinyl
- Heat transfer vinyl
- Permanent vinyl
- Infusible ink transfer sheets
- Textured paper

- Embossed cardstock

Strong Grip Machine Mat:

(Cricut Strong Grip Mat)

This is the purple color mat. This is meant for heavy-duty materials. Examples of such materials are:

- Balsa and Basswood
- Chipboard
- Magnetic sheets
- Leather
- Glitter cardstock
- Wood sheets
- Thick cardstock

Care and Longevity of the Mat:

The mats are expensive, so you might be interested in keeping them in use for a long while. The only way to increase a mat's life is to use it carefully and take good care of it. Here are a few pointers regarding the care procedure for these mats:

- Always replace the transparent cover/film on the mat after usage. This will protect the mat from unnecessary dirt and dust.
- After every use, a lint roller over the mat surface to get rid of any material residue.
- Clean the mat with non-alcoholic wipes.
- Except for the fabric mat, wash your mats with soapy water. The fabric mat is different from all the other mats and cannot be cleaned with water.
- Except for the fabric mat, use a scraper to remove all material residue to clear the mat surface.

Chapter 2. Design Space Software

The most significant aspect of designing projects is construction space. The basic program in which all the templates and layouts for cutting is produced is Design Space. You need to go to the Cricut website first and then download the Design Space software. For both your desktop and other Android and iOS devices, this service is made available. After download, you must sign up with the Cricut and build a personalized account. Now, you are set for your first creation.

For some, knowing about a new application may be an overwhelming activity. The Design Space, however, is a consumer-friendly program. The interface is simple and straightforward. However, before beginning any project, it is often best to understand Dthe applications. The program will be needed for all projects on the Cricut Makar. so, before getting into a project, it is necessary to have previous knowledge about the software. Design Space is described, step-by-step with illustrations in the following chapter to make it easier for you to comprehend.

The Design Space Home Page

(Homepage Layout)

The first page is the Design Space as you open the app. The homepage has four parts. The topmost being the header, then the banner, which has all the Cricut promotions and offers. The other two sections are my designs and the featured material.

Four Sections of Homepage

Here is a detailed description of the Design Space Homepage. All four parts will be explained in depth.

- The Header
- The Banner
- My Projects Section
- Featured Projects

The Header

On the left side is the menu icon. This has two options, the homepage, and the canvas. This icon helps you to switch from homepage to canvas and then back. Apart from switching

32

between the homepage and canvas, this menu also has other function options.

- New Machine Setup
- Print then Cut Calibration
- Manage Custom Materials
- Update filmware
- Account details
- Link Cartridges
- Cricut Access
- Settings
- Legal
- New Features
- Country Selection
- Help

As Design Space is the software used for all the other Cricut machines, you need to set up your new machine from here. Any calibration required is adjusted with the cut, then print calibration. You can manage your account settings. The Cricut Access icon is for the subscription. The settings icon is for your canvas setting selection. You can select your country, and there is a Help icon with a lot of frequently asked questions and their answers.

The Banner

This space is for Cricut advertisements and promotions. Any news about new accessories, ongoing promotions, deals, and offers are advertised here.

My Projects

This place will be blank when you first start. When you make and save a project, it will be stored in this area. All your projects will be profiled in this area in order of recent to oldest. This will make it easy for you to scan all your projects and repeat another project if you want to.

Featured Projects

This area will show you all the projects that Cricut provides you which are ready to make. In these files, you must select a file and click make it, and the rest will be guided to you. All the materials, design, blades, and the order in which the materials must be cut, all will be guided to you through Design Space.

The Canvas Layout

To get to the canvas from the home page. There are three locations where you can get to the canvas. the picture has highlighted all those three locations:

(How to reach the canvas)

The Canvas Layout

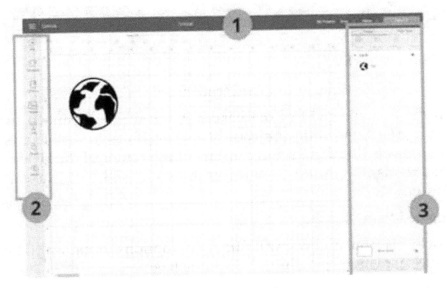

(Canvas Lyout)

When you open the Canvas, this is divided into four major parts. In this chapter, we will discuss all these four parts in detail. We will walk you through each part separately, and hopefully, you will be at east towards the end of the chapter. Once you understand all these parts, you will be ready for your first project. The canvas screen is divided into the following parts:

- The Header and Edit Panel
- The Insert Menu for Project
- The Menu for Layers
- The Creative Field or Main Canvas

Header and Edit Panel

Design Space Canvas page's top region is essentially divided into two sections.

Header

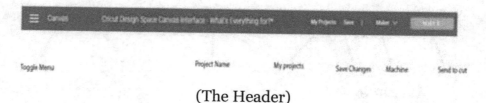

Toggle Menu   Project Name   My projects   Save Changes   Machine   Send to cut

(The Header)

In the extreme right of the header is the toggle menu. In the center, the name of the project will appear. If you have not saved the project, Untitled Project appears at the center of the header. On the right side are the system selection and the 'Make It' button.

Toggle Menu

Click this icon, and you will find a new options dropdown. This is the same menu you find on the homepage.

Project Name

In the center of the header will be displayed the project name. Until you name your project, Untitled project is written in this space. You can name a project only after you have inserted one image or text into the canvas space.

Type of Machine

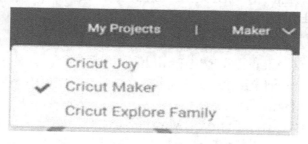

(Cricut Machine Selection)

As the Design Space is used for all the Cricut Machines, it is essential to select Cricut Maker from this dropdown. As some functions are exclusive to the Cricut Maker, if you have not selected the Cricut Maker, you will not see those functions displayed in the design space.

36

Make It

When you are done designing, save your files and upload them. Next, click on Make It. After this, you will have to select the correct blades and materials for cutting. All the guidelines will be given to you by design space regarding what to place on the mats and which material must be cut first if you are working with more than one material.

Below the header is the Edit Panel. It is to edit and organize components. You can select what sort of font might be suitable for the project using this panel. This is a taskbar where a lot of options are present. You might get a bit overwhelmed, but the functions and icons are straightforward to use once you get the hang of it.

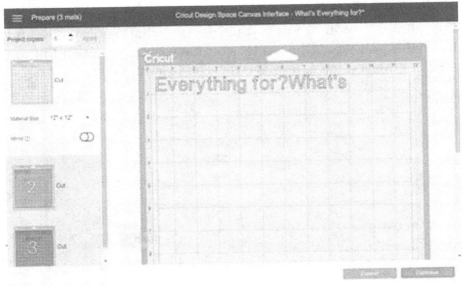

(Prepare Screen for Project Layers)

The Edit Panel

The resizing, text addition, alignment of projects, addition, and deletion of shapes and fonts, redo, and undo, all on the canvas, can be controlled at this Edit panel. A full description of each part is explained in the whole chapter.

(Edit Toolbar)

1.Redo, Undo Icon

We often make errors when working. These icons are a perfect way to fix mistakes. When an error is made, press Undo. Whenever you unintentionally remove something , press the Redo icon to get it back.

2.Fill, Linetype Icon

This choice would inform your device what equipment and the blades you would be using. you have options depending on the machine you have, in this case, The Cricut Maker.

Linetype

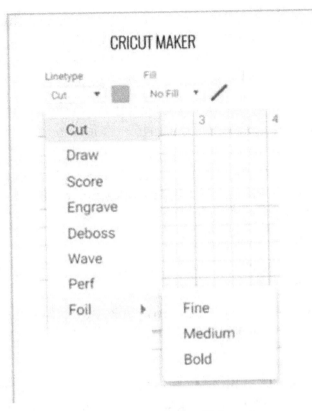

(Linetype and Fill Icon)

Here you will choose the type of blade you will use for this project. In the Cricut Maker, you have the most number of options. you can choose to Cut, Score, Deboss, Wave, Foil, Perforate, Draw or Engrave

Here is an in-depth description of all these options:

Cut Option

The default setting is the Cut option for the Cricut Maker. When this option is selected, whatever you will put on the canvas will be cut when you press 'Make It'. so if your intention is to use another function, be sure to change the setting.

Draw Option

If you want to draw out your designs, you can use this option. When you choose this option, you have to load the Cricut Markers and Pens into the markets sockets provided in the Machine. Remember, the Cricut Maker dose not color your projects.

Scoring Option

The Cricut Maker has a special scoring tip for this function.

This option is useful to make boxes and greeting cards. If you require the project to fold, you can use this tool to score on the lines where the folding is going to take place. this helps your project to have perfect finish.

Deboss Option

Deboss means to press in the material. This is exactly what the deboss tip does.

this function can be used on cardstock and other lightweight materials. this is to beautify your crafts like cards and boxes.

Engrave Option

viIt helps to engrave numerous kinds of materials. This option can be used to engrave monograms and designs on aluminum sheets and other vinyl sheets.

Wave Option

This option is a part of the speciality tips of the Cricut Maker. If you want to make your project with wavy edges, you can use this option. this is ideal for cards, cake toppers, name takes and invites.

Foil Option

this is a decorative option. Can be mostly used to decorate greeting cards, make beautiful monograms and beautify different materials with gold and silver tint. There are speciality gold and silver foil sheets compatible with Cricut Maker which are used for this function.

Perforating Option

This is useful if your project involves making tear out sheets. You can make ticket sheets and vouchers with this function.

Fill

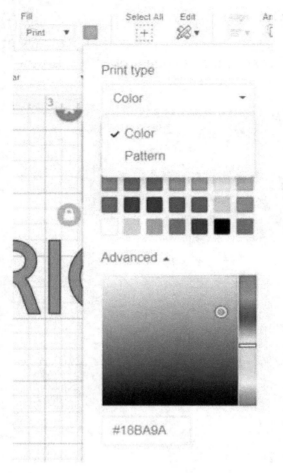

(Fill Icon)

This option is used for printing. this is only available when the cutting linetype is selected. if you choose no fill, it means that only cutting has to done. If you choose the fill option, it means you have to cut as well as print your project. You used your home printer for the printing work and the Cricut Maker for cutting this project.

3. Select All Option

This is a very simple and useful option. If you want to pick up and transfer your whole project at once, you click this option and everything on the canvas will be selected.

4. Editing Option

When you click the Edit Icon, you see a drop down with several options. Cut, copy, paste, duplicate. You can use all these options to cut objects and put somewhere else on the canvas. You can repeat an object or shape you want to cut multiple times in the project.

5. Align Option

(Align Icon)

This option is used to determine where your project will be centered on the canvas. You have different options how to align your project on the canvas.

Align Left: If you choose this option, all the components of the project will be directed from the left side of the canvas. Meaning that the orientation of the project will be left.

Align Correct: If you choose this option, the entire project will be of right orientation.

Center Horizontal: This option is mostly used for photographs. When you choose this, all the components will be oriented horizontally.

Center Vertically: Horizontal: This option aligns all the project components vertical in column form.

Align Top: According to this orientation, the components will be set on the top most part of the canvas.

Align Bottom: If you choose this option, all the components will be aligned to tthe bottom of the canvas.

Center Align: When you select this option, the entire project will be placed in the center of the canvas perfectly.

Distribute: This option is used for spacing between all the elements on the canvas. If you have several objects and cannot space them equally, you select this option to perfectly space all the items. You can space the objects both ways, either horizontally or vertically.

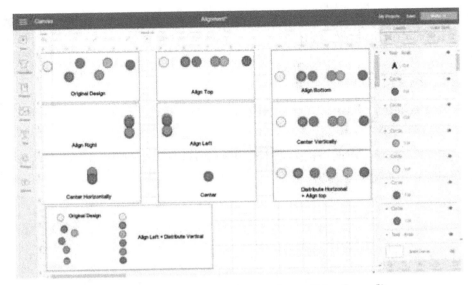

(Different Allignment Options Displayed)

6. Arranging Option

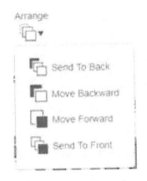

(Arrange Icon)

This function is useful if you have multiple componets on your canvas. Like text, pictures and shapes. This option help you to determine the correct sequence of the componets from top to bottom. with this you will select which component is bottom most and which is top most. Which component goes in the back and which is on the front. You can organize your components according to your design. You have four options. you select each components and arrange them by these four options

Send to Back: Selection of this will make the selected element to transfer to the back of all the other components.

Jump Backward: This option will make the component selected will move one layer back.

Going Ahead : This option will make the component selected to move one layer ahead.

Send to Front: With this option, the component will be placed at the foremost position.

7.Flip Option

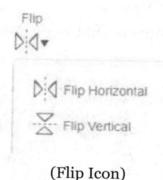

(Flip Icon)

This option creates a reflection of the selected component. There are two options, the image can be flipped either horizontally or vertically.

8. Size Option

This is to size the components of your project. When you click a component and click size and select self, you can manually adjust the size of each component you need to cut. There is a little lock sign that actually locks the dimensions of the components. When you click that lock, it means that you want to change the dimensions.

9.Rotate Option

This option is used to move a certain object towards a certain angle. it can also be used to rotate the object on the canvas at a 180 degree angle or full 360 degree angle.

10.Position Option

This option can be used to position items at a certain place on the canvas. The function is very much like the alignment option but used for more sophetication. this can be used to position single objects through the canvas.

11.Font Option

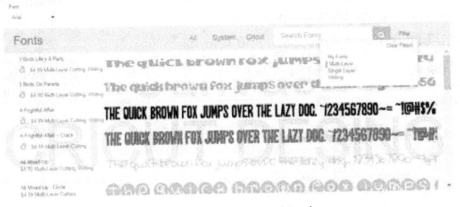

(Font Icon and Options)

You choose this option to add text to your canvas. Some of the fonts are free to use but for some fonts, you have to pay or subscribe to Cricut Access.

12. Style Option

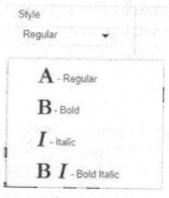

(Style Icon)

With this option you can turn your fort to either bold, italic or both. Depends on your own choice.

13. Letter space, font space and line space

This option is used to modify your text. The size of the text can be modified, the space between the letters and the space between different words.

14. Alignment Option

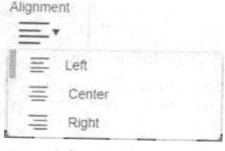

(Alignment Icon)

This option is for the text only. If you have a paaragraph or few sentences of text to be cut, you might want to align. The alignment can be either left, center or right.

15.Curve Option

This is a creative option for the text as well. This option has a sliger which is set in the middle. If you move it to the left you will form a rainbow style word alignment. If you move to right, the text will be arranged in the downward direction. If you move to the right most direction, the text will be arranged in a circle form.

16. Advance Option

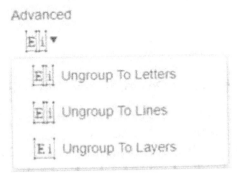

(Advanced Icon)

This option is also for the text on the canvas. This is a drop-down option and you see different options.

Ungroup to Letters: If you want to customize each of your text letter, you can use this option. This option will let you separate every letter in a different layer.

Ungroup to Lines: This option is similar to the ungroup to letters option. The only difference is that it applies to each text sentence or line. If you want to modify each sentence in your paragraph you can use this function.

Ungroup to Layers: This option applies on the multi-layer fonts. These fonts are either available with the Cricut Access subscription or the font usage is individually purchased.

Left Panel

(Left panel of Design Space Highlighted)

In the left panel you can start a new project, view your previous ventures, find photographs and designs for creating a new project. Lets discuss all the options in the panel one by one.

New Button:

to start a new project you click this button and you have a blank canvas.

Template Button:

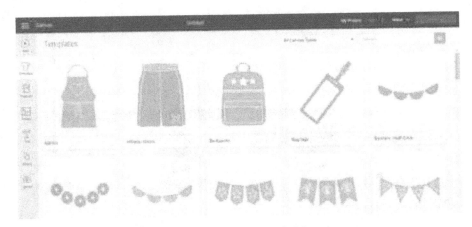

(Template Display)

The Design Space provides you with a number of generic templates to start a new project. This will serve as a project outline or a mock up. You have alot of options for templates like banners, tags, labels, aprons, T-shirts, shorts etc.

Projects Button:

Projects

(Projects Page)

This option has all the projects you have already made. If you have to make a project again, you can easily select the file and press make it. No hassle at all. All the ready made projects from Cricut are also available to make here. If you subscribe to Cricut Access, you will be able to access a wide variety of ready made projects to make.

Images Button:

Images

From here you can find a huge variety of images and photo files to cut. There are images already present with the Design Space. But to gain access to much more images, you will have to subscribe to Cricut Access. The photos and images you will upload yourself as well will appear here.

Text Button:

This is a fairly simple button. You click here and a window appears on the canvas where you can add your text. Then to select the font, style, size, and everything else about the text can be controlled and designed by the top taskbar.

Shapes Button

To add simple shapes to your design you click this option. All the basic shapes are given. You can create more intricate designs using these simple shapes. You can adjust the sizes and use more than one shape for your project.

Score Button:

This is a very useful function. This is most useful if you are making cards and boxes which need to be folded after cutting. It is mostly used on light weight materials like the cardstock. When you apply this option on a design, the scoring blade will score along the lines in your design which have to be folded.

Upload button:

Upload

If you want to upload an image for your design you can press upload and select the image from your device. The Design Space software will guide you how to properly upload to use the specific images.

Right Panel – Layers

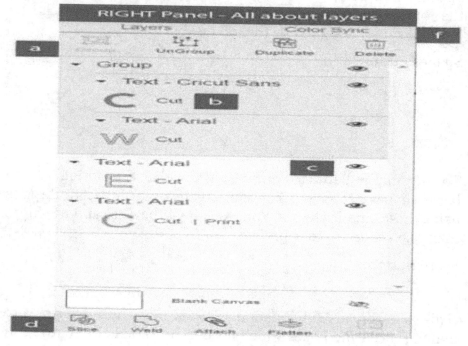

(Right Panel Icons)

This is an interesting part of the project. So, what are layers? Layers in the Cricut world represent each different component or material used in the project on the canvas. So a simple project may have one or two layers and a more complexed project might have five or six layers depending on the design.

54

You can take an example of a birthday card. So it will have some text, some shapes on the card and the card itself. Now each of these separate component is a layer.

Mostly each component or layer can be edited or modified but there are some files like the JPEG and PNG images, that cannot be edited. The function of the Layers Function is described in detail.

a. Grouping, Ungrouping, Duplicating and Removing

On the layers panel on the top you will find these options.

To Group:

This option is used if you want to make some components of the project as a same layer, or you want those specific components to stick together, you select all the parts and group them together. It can be either only shapes or can be shapes and text. More than one part of the project can be integrated into a single layer.

To Ungroup:

As the name suggests, this means to remore a certain component from a group. Suppose that you want a shape or text to be represented as a separate layer, you choose that component and ungroup it from the other components. Sometimes it is also done to modify or resize a certain part of a group and then can be again regrouped in a single layer.

To Duplicate:

This option creates a copy of an already designed layer. Any layer or design you want to repeat in the same project you cn use this option.

To Delete:

Tis option is very straightforward. If you think a part of the project is not required or has to be removes, the delete option is used.

b. Linetype and Fill

With this option you will choose the linetype for each of the layer. Linetype means that the function to be used to cut the project. Either it has to be cut, or perforated, or scored or be cut in waves aor the project has to be foiled. In this option, you select the function for each layer.

c. Visibility of Layers

On the canvas, each layer has a tiny eye on the side. When you click that eye, the layer will be disappear. A tiny cross will appear at that space. This option is helpful when you want to see each layer separately.

d. Blank Canvas

This option changes the color of the canvas. The canvas is actually white in color. Sometimes you wish to see your designs with a different background. So for that you can change the color of canvas to see the effect. You can use this option on templates as well. If your design is created on templates, you can change the color of templates to see the affect.

e. To Slice, to weld, to attach, to flatten and to contour

All these functions are very useful and are self explanatory from their names.

To Slice:

If you wish to separate a part of text or shape from a design, you select that part or shape and click slice. That part will be separated form the design and you can place is whereever you want to place on the canvas.

To Weld:

To weld is the total opposite of slice. If you want to merge two parts of a design you can use this function. You select both the parts and click weld, and those parts you selected will be merged. This can result in the formation of a whole new design.

To Attach:

This function is like the grouping function, only more stronger. If you select two shapes and click attach both the components will attach and change color. The attached result will take the color of the layer that is on the back. These components will remain intact for the cutting process as well.

To Flatten:

This option is only applicable when you select from no fill to print option. It mans that you have to print then cut design. So if you want to print multiple layers together, you select all of them and then click flatten and can print them together.

To contour:

This option is utilized if you want to leave out parts of the design. Suppose you do not want certain parts of the project. You select those parts and contour them out. The only thing to note is that this option is only available for shapes and designs that has elements which can be contoured or left out.

f. Color Sync

On the design on your canvas, there is a different color representing each material. Now if you need all these shades in your design it is okay. But if you have multiple shades of suppose blue or yellow, you might want to sync them into the same shade. So you click and then drag the color you want to remove and put it on the color you want.

The Main Canvas Area

Here is the space where all the magic takes place. All the functions described in the entire chapter are applied on the canvas. Canvas is the actual place where the designing and creating takes place. We will discuss further the layout of the canvas.

Rulers and Grid of Canvas

The whole canvas is divided into a grid with the x and y axis. The default measurement setting of the grid is in inches. You can also change it to centimeters. The grid gives you an idea and visualization of the project and the size. This grid can be called the visual or digital representation of the Cricut Mats.

Selection

(Main Canvas)

On the canvas each layer is represented with a blue box outlining it. You can select that box and can edit the layer or design in the right panel for layers. On each box on the upper left corner is a tiny cross. If you wnt to delete the layer you can press that button.

On the right corner is a curved arrow. You can tilt or rotate the design with the help of this. In the bottom left corner is a small lock. This is supposed to keep the design and image with in proportion. This if, unlocked can make the image disproportional. So it is better not to unlock this option. In the bottom right corner is the option to modify the size of the design.

Cricut Access

A lot of people when starting out with the Cricut Maker get very confused between the Design Space and Cricut Access. There is a simple difference, Design Space is the downloadable software that all current Cricut Machines use for designing and cutting projects. Whereas the Cricut Access is a subscription plan of Cricut. This is a paid service that enables you to use ready made Cricut projects, more than 400 types of texts and 100, 000 images. Not only this, when you subscribe with Cricut Access, you get discount of 10 percent on all your Cricut merchandise. Even when you buy sale items you get an additional 10 percent off. As a member of the Cricut Access community, you get a priority status with your orders being jumped up above the non-subscribers. The Cricut Access subscription provides you free shipping for all your orders. It is worth noting that the Design Space provides some free fonts and images as well as some free to use ready to make projects. When you first time register with Design Space, you get a free Cricut Access trial subscription. But you cannot save any image or font of the Cricut Access for use when your subscription is expired. Cricut offers monthly and yearly packages for Cricut Access that can be monthly or yearly renewed. You can directly cancel your subscription at any time.

Chapter 3. Business Ideas for the Cricut Maker

With the advent of the online market places and the popularity of personalized products, small businesses' scope has increased. In this chapter, some ideas to start a business with your creativity and the Cricut Maker are given. There are few universal rules for a good business. Those rules are discussed as follows:

- To start any business a person has to be very patient and very hard working. These are the core rules to become a successful business person. There is no short cut or no easy money scheme. Only hardwork pays off. So if you are thinking of starting your own business, you need to understand that it is going to take time and hardwork to take off. Another golden rule for any business is to create your niche.
- You might have heard the saying, jack of all trades, master of none. This saying applys to most businesses. If you try to do everything at once you will soon become exhausted and loose hope. You need to focus on one thing and create your short term and lon term goals to achive these goals.
- Next most important rule to launch a successful business is to create a product of good quality. People tend to pay a lot of money for good quality product. You can earn more than market price if your product quality is exceptional. Along with being exceptional, your quality should also be consistent. We see a lot of products where the initial quality is good and subsequently it declines.
- In today's age, one of the most important quality of a good business persin is to have networking and marketing skills. The best way to market your product is online and through social media. You have to be very digitally smart to create a successful business online. Market your product on all social media sites. Make tutorials. People

tend to buy products which they no about. Create elaborate vedious and tutorials for your products.

With all this wisdom you are perfectly ready to create your very own Cricut Crafts Business. Following are few ideas that might help you stary your business. Best of luck.

Vinyl Stickers and Decals

(Beautiful Decals)

One of the easiest things you can make is vinyl stickers and decals if you own a Cricut Maker. They are in demand, easy to make, and a lot of capital will not be required to start such a business. You can offer to make customized stickers and decals for special occasions as well. Vinyl decals are a very popular thing now a days. You can offer to make decals for the windows. A lot of people these days avoid using curtains for their windows because of dust and allergies. The prefer to cover the windows with decals. You can make different custom sized window decals. A lot of people order for decals for labelling items. For organizing an office or pantry. Youc can create office shelfing decals or pantry organizing decals and sell them online. You can offer creative designs and shapes for these decals. Another idea for decals is different animals and characters for kids. A lot of parents want to decorate their kids rooms with creative options but don't want to spend a lot of money. You can use this as your niche. Create elaborate designs for kids. Cartoon borders for kids room walls. Animal pronts for their windows. Big pictures of colorful animals and plants. Maybe you can offer to make a whole jungle theme for kids rooms. Different thesmes for girls and boys rooms. Thw best thing about this business is that it can be started form the comfort of your own home. The initial investment is also very low. The only thing you will have to work on is your networking and marketing. To get your product to your customers. Work on your networking skills. Market your product everywhere. Use your product yourself. This will be the best publicity. Initially gift your creative product to your friends and family and create awareness about your product in your circle. Positive word of mouth is also very good publicity.

To Get Started:

To start this business, you will need:

- Cricut Maker
- Suitable Vinyl Sheets
- Suitable Mats
- Packaging and posting supplies.

Advantages:

- Low to start the business
- You can start with a small project
- Easy to make
- Do not take a lot of space to setup
- In demand all around the year
- Easy to ship as lightweight

Disadvantages

- The profit rates are low

Custom Mugs, T-Shirts, Tote Bags

(Different Mugs designed with Cricut Maker)

This is a very lucrative business idea. You can make customized and personalized products. You can also make mugs and T-shirts with quirky and exciting phrases and quotes. This can prove to be a very successful business. For this business aswell, networking is the key. If you decide to make t-shirts. Wear those shirts. If someone asks about them, be confident in telling all about those shirts. People love confident people who know what they are talking about. Talk about the quality of material you used. The designs you can offer. How early you can deliver. This is all part of your marketing strategy. A business person is always sure of their product. Know your product inside out. Also use good materials if you are into making clothes. People would pay high prives for good quality fabric. Low quality fabric will not be durable and will create a negative affect for your product. Also be creative with your designs. In todays world people love memes and quirky quotes. Create funny hash tag t-shirts. Be creative with colors. People tend to buy things that are stricking and catchy to the eye.

Similarly if you want to make mugs and cups. Be creative. Use colors. Use the sentiments of people. Your work of art should connect with people. It should make them think about their loved ones. It should make them laugh. It should make them nostalgic. If your art work ignites emothin, if will definitely click with the consumer.

Also with this business, people would want to invest because they will be getting a ready made product. These products make for beautiful gifts aswell. So, you might have high sales in the holiday seasons.

The only drawback to start this business is that the investment cost is high and you will need a bigger space to start this business.

To Get Started:

To start this business, you will need:

- Cricut Maker
- Transfer Vinyl Sheets
- Infusable Ink sheets
- Blank mugs, T-shirts, and tote bags
- Appropriate mats for cutting
- Cricut Easy Press 2
- Packaging and posting materials

Advantages:

- Easy to make
- Market value is higher as it is a finished product
- The profit is higher
- The business has scope all year long

Disadvantages:

- The initial investment is higher
- A bigger space is needed for operations

Giving Cricut Tutorials

A lot of people are investing in the Cricut Maker these days. Though it is easy to use, people find it difficult to read how-to books and manuals. People find it easier to watch a video or get in-person tutorials. You can start a vlog or a tutorial class. You can charge for your tutorial classes. In both ways, you can create an income. By teaching your skill to others you will be able to better your craft aswell as be more confident. A lot of times people who see your vedios or tutorials would want to buy your creative products aswell. This can also be a source of income. You and offer discounts on your tutorial classes such as take one class is 10 dollars but if you book 5 classes you will have to pay 40 dollars. This way you can attract more students to your class. You can advertise your tutorial classes on all social media sites. Another strategy you can use is that you give one class free and the subsequent classes you will charge. People love ti try free classes and tutorials. But if you are successful to get them hooked, then they might aswell join your class. This is not easy but definitely worth it.

To Get Started:

- Cricut Maker
- A video recorder
- A designated space to shoot your videos
- Expertise in editing videos
- All the craft supplies for the crafts you teach

Advantages:

- Can provide tutorials from the comfort of your home
- No initial investment is required
- You get to showcase your creativity

Disadvantages

- Low scope for earnings until you get more students or followers

Party Decorations

(Halowwen Decorations Made by Cricut Maker)

There is a trend to have theme parties these days. People want supplies and decorations like name tags, decorations, give away boxes, cake toppers, etc according to a theme. You can create a business making party decorations and supplies for all kinds of events. All year round, there are birthdays, anniversaries, weddings, bridal, and baby showers. You will never run out of business. This business is for someone who is really creative. Because there is a lot of competition in this field. A lot of event planners charge a lot of money to create theme parties and events. But affordability is a huge issue among people. Everyone wants a lavish party but not all can afford. So you can create personalized party items and sell them at a lower cost than the event planners. This business has a lot of scpe but still a lot of competition is there in this business. The good thing about this business is that the investment costs are low. Also there are personal event all year round so you still can attract a lot of cutomers with your product. This business follows the same rule. If you provide good quality, people will come to you for services. If you are able to offer superior quality than your competitors at a reasonable price, people will pay for your product.

To Get Started:

- Cricut Maker
- Different types of cardstock
- Cutting Mat
- Packaging and postage supplies

Advantages

- Low cost to start the business

Greeting Cards

(Different decorations and Greeting Cards for Chrismas)

Greeting cards are very much in demand, especially during the holiday season. People love to send personalized greeting cards to friends and family. Handcrafted cards have a very personal touch. But not all people have the time or creativity to design and make such greeting cards, so they would want to invest in some handcrafted cards online. This can be started as a seasonal business. The only problem with this business is that it can only flourish in the holiday season. With the digitalization of the whole world, the demand fro cards is declining by the day. However, in the holiday season, there are some people who are old school and still want to follow the old time tradition of sending and exchanging greeting cards, Such old school people will also pay good money for creative and heartfelt greeting cards. So if you plan to start this buiseness, you must create something which connects with the peoples emotions. It has been earlier said in this book to connect with the peoples' emotions. Why is there stress on connecting with people at an emotional level? Because creativity cannot be quantified. Creative businesses always have to connect with peoples' emotions and sensibilities to work.

To Get Started:

- Cricut Machine
- Different types of cardstock
- Decorative materials
- Cutting Mats
- Glue
- Postage and packaging materials

Advantages:

- Easy to make
- The initial investment is low
- Can be sold in bulk
- High rates of profits in the holiday season

Disadvantages:

- The profits can only be gained during holiday seasons

Stuffed Toys

(Creative Stuffed Animal)

Stuffed animals can make beautiful gifts. They can be equally interesting to give to adults as well as children. With the Cricut Maker, you can now easily cut fabric, so this will be a great idea. The Design Space has many free stuffed animal ready made cutting projects. All you have to do is create the finished product out of those designs. You can sell these cuties online for a fair price. This can prove to be a lucrative small business. These stuffed animals are a great gift for babies and kids. Most of the time when we want to gift something to a kid we rely on stuffed animals. The reason being that for other gift items we will have to get the specifics right. For examole if we want to gift a kid clothes, we need to know the exact size. If we want to gift a baby some baby products, we will have to be sensitive about their parents' preferences. In this regard stuffed animals are a great gift. People also want products which are different form the regularly available items. This desire to stand out leads people to invest in handmade and personalized products.

So, for a business, this is a very good idea. These stuffed animals are easy to make and require less time and effort. Fabric and fillings are relatively reasonable to purchase if you buy in bulk. A good idea would be to stick to 2 to 3 styles of stuffed animals when you start your business.

To Get Started:

To get started you will need:

- Cricut Maker
- Suitable Fabric
- Suitable stuffing
- Fabric Grip Mat
- Sewing Machine
- Sewing supplies
- Packing And Posting Supplies

Advantages

- A high rate of profit from buyers if the product is of good quality
- Not a lot of competition
- High purchases during the holiday season

Disadvantages:

- High cost to start the business
- Need a large space for working

Creative Hairbands

(Kid wearing a headband made with Cricut Maker)

Hairbands are very much in demand right now. Mostly these are popular among toddlers and babies, but women of all ages use them. So these products are in demand among women of all ages. Headbands and head pieces have made a huge comeback these days. For little girls they can prove to be a perfect gift. If you plan to make these headbands, they will prove to be cost effective as less material is used and you can sell it at higher prices because people tend to spend much on their kids and on kids girfting. You can create four or five generic designs and can sell them as a bundle. A good idea would be to select a single design and cut out in four or dive common colors and sell them as a pack. Mothers and aunts of little girls would love to buy such stuff. When creating stuff for toddlers and children be very careful to create stuff with soft materials, if the material will be stiff or hard, they will be useless for kids and no one will buy them.

You can also make headbands for adults as they are very much in fashion. With headbands for girls and ladies you can experiment with more materials and textures. You can even use embelishmets with the headbands. You can even create embellishments with a cricut maker. Headbands with embellishmets can be sold at a higher price.

These are relatively easy to make. Low cost to make and can be stored in a smaller space. Due to them being lightweight, shipping is also easy.

To Get Started:

To get started you will need

- Cricut Maker
- Fabric
- Sewing Machine
- Sewing Supplies
- Packaging and postage supplies

Advantages:

- This product is high in demand
- Sales are high throughout the year
- Scope for profit is high
- The initial cost to start the project is not very high.

Disadvantages:

- A lot of competition already there in the market place.

Keychains

(A Creative Keychain)

With the Cricut Maker, it is possible to cut materials such as leather and wood. This allows you to create unique keychains. People are very fond of fun and quirky key chains. Keychains can be sold online for a fair price. The good thing about keychans is that it can be sold to men and women both. They are not gender restrictive. With keychins also, people want to stand out with their unique style. If you want to create designs for men and women both, you have to target at both of them. One way is to create unisex designs and the other way is to create two different types of products. This depends entirely on you, how you want to target your consumer and what works for you. Whatever style you choose, you will have to be extremely creative. One thing is worth mentioning, leather is a very popular material for keychains. This also gives a very sophisticated effect. Leather products can be sold at a higher price. So, you might consider making leather keychains.

To Get Started:

To get started, you need:

- Cricut Maker

- Strong Grip Cutting Mat
- Knife blade
- Materials for the keychain (wood or leather)
- Keyrings
- Packaging and postage supplies

Advantages

- Easy to create
- Can be sold for a reasonable price
- Easy to ship as it is a lightweight product

Disadvantages:

- The startup cost is relatively high.
- The materials for the keychain are expensive

Paper Flower Bouquets

(Bouqet made of paper Flowers)

Real flowers are very expensive. The tend to wilt soon as well. But you need flower bouquets for all occasions and especially for gifting. Flowers are a huge part of weddings. Everyone wants their wedding to look like a fairytale wedding. But sometimes our pockets don't allow that kind of luxury. In weddings people look for alternatives of real flowers and paper crafted flowers are a decent substitute. Paper flowers, if created correctly, look verymuch like real flowers. People would invest in real looking paper flowers. If you can create a good quality product, this business can gain a lot of profits. The condition for success in this business is quality and price. If you can provide an exceptional quality at a competitive price, your business can take off. The drawback of this business is the level of concentration it requires to create each flower. The amount of work required to create even a single flower. For such kinds of bouquets to look real, each flower has to be cerated by connecting separate petals. This requires a high level of precision and a lot of patience to create each flower. You need to be very cerative to design a whole bouquet. Sometimes when you create a flower, it looks very beautiful individually but doesn't look as appealing when a part of a bouqet. So, it is important to actually create beautiful flowers as well as intricate designs for the bouquet. So, if you are not passionate enough for this level of perfection, this business might not be for you. But, if you are enthusiastic about something like this, go for it by all means.

To Get Started:

To get started you will need:

- Cricut Maker
- Standard and Light Grip Mat
- Crepe paper
- Thin and thick cardstock
- Different colored paper
- glue
- flower wire
- wirecutter
- scissors

- Packing Materials
- Postage Materials

Advantages

- The margin for profit is high
- This is a booming business, and there is not a lot of competition

Disadvantages:

- Challenging to ship due to size and fragility
- A high-quality product is required
- Time-consuming to create individual bouquets

Chapter 4. DIY Cricut Maker Projects

Pantry Project

Now, by this point, it has already been established that you are a creative person, but are you a super organized person as well? If the answer to this question is yes, you would love to have your pantry organized. And what pantry can be organized without labels? Worry no more; here you have a simple step by step project to create labels for your pantry jars and bottles. The following DIY project is about kitchen labels. These labels go well with clear canisters as well as solid-colored ones. One tip to make the labels would be that we do not design labels for patterned boxes and containers. This will create an untidy finish. It is also recommended that you should have uniform containers for organizing. This gives a clean look and motivates you to keep the pantry organized because of its visual effect on your mind.

In this tutorial, label making is directed towards making them for the kitchen containers. But you can use the same tutorial to create labels for other organization projects as well. You can label your crafts closet and containers with these labels. If you are a teacher, you might want to create labels for your supply closet. In short, the possibilities are unlimited. Let us get started with this straightforward and basic project to create labels.

(Kitchen Jars with Cricut Labels)

- Cricut Maker Project Level: Easy (Beginner)
- Time: Start to finish – 2 hours approximately.
- Materials and Supplies:
    - Cricut Maker Machine
    - Premium Fine Point Blade
    - Cricut Removable Vinyl
    - Cricut Transfer Tape
    - Design Space Software
    - Cricut Access
    - Cricut Toolkit
    - Cricut Scraper Tool
    - Cricut Standard Grip Mat
- Instructions:

1. First, you must have a cleared, decluttered space whenever you start any project. Then you collect all the supplies you are going to require in the project. Only after that, you must start your project.
2. Next, measure out what size you require for labels. This step is essential. It will help if you determine what size labels you want for your jars and containers. If you skip this step, there are chances that the labels would come out larger or smaller than necessary. So please do not miss this step.
3. Next, open your Design Space on your laptop or any other device you prefer to use.
4. Go to the canvas page. On the left panel, click the New option. Now, you will have a clear canvas.
5. After this, you have two options, either select from the already given projects and customize them according to your requirement, or you do it manually. It is often suggested that you make your first few projects by selecting the already made projects. But here, the manual method is explained.
6. The first step will be to choose the template. You easily click the template button and choose the appropriate template which will be for labeling.
7. Next, go to the text. Choose your preferred font and type out all the labels. Adjust the font size.
8. When you are satisfied with your labels, click the "Make It" button.
9. After clicking the 'Make It" button, the software might align all the labels differently than you typed out. Do not worry. This alignment will be to use the materials most effectively.
10. After this, the software will give you commands to arrange everything in order before it starts cutting.
11. For this project, you will install the Premium Fine point blade.
12. Next, you will stick the vinyl sheet to the cutting Mat.

13. When all is adequately aligned, install the Mat to the Cricut Maker. It will start cutting now.
14. You must wait till the Cricut completes cutting.
15. Next is the fun part. The process of weeding. First, you take out the Mat from the Cricut Maker. Remove your vinyl from the grip mat. Use a hook tool to weed out all the excess space, only leaving the text. Be incredibly careful because this process needs attention and precision. Before starting to weed, you can also cut the labels in rectangles or the required shape. It will take time and concentration to weed all the labels.
16. Now only the text and the backing piece of vinyl are left. All the unnecessary vinyl has already been weeded.
17. Next comes the transfer tape. Carefully cut the transfer tape according to the size of the labels. Now peel off one side of the transfer tape and push it down on the label. Use the Cricut scraper tool to press on the transfer tape properly. Repeat this process with each label.
18. This must be done with precision to give a neat finish.
19. The next step is to carefully pull back the transfer tape from the backing material. Ensure that the entire text of the label comes off with the transfer tape when you pull up.
20. Next, stick the label directly to the container. Before pressing it hard, check that the placement is correct. When you are sure of the placement, use the Cricut scraping tool to press the label against the jar or bottle for firm adherence.
21. Repeat the process with each label.

Outdoor Welcome Mat

A thing about crafters and creative people is that they have this desire to showcase their work. They love praise. They want their work to be displayed for people to see and appreciate. If you are one of those, this project is for you. What else is better than placing your piece of art right at your doorstep. As soon as someone is about to enter your house, they will see this unique piece and will stop to ask where you got it from, and you can proudly announce that this is my creation. This project is a simple and elegant welcome mat to be placed outside your doorstep. You can modify this project and make an elaborate piece. But for beginners, it is recommended to first get practice with the easier stuff. Easier stuff will be made quickly and boost your sense of achievement. When you complete a few easy projects successfully, you will be confident enough to graduate to the next level. For now, you might want to try this simple DIY Cricut project.

- Cricut Maker Project Level: Easy (Beginner)
- Time: Start to finish- 3 hours approximately
- Materials and Supplies:
  - Cricut Maker
  - Standard Grip Cutting Mat
  - Premium Fine Point Blade
  - Cricut Removable Vinyl
  - Cricut Toolset
  - Navy Blue Craft paint (weather resistant)
  - Foam paintbrush (with round tip)
  - Coir Rug
- Instructions
1. It is always useful to clean up your space before starting any project. Just clear up your space and collect all the materials and supplies you would need for the project.
2. First, measure your Mat and determine the size of the text you want to place on the Mat.
3. Open Design Space on your laptop or the device of your choice. Go straight to the canvas and start a new project.
4. Next, click the text button. The text toolbar will appear on the top of the page.

5. You can choose your favorite font, adjust the size, and type your text. It can be something as simple as hello.
6. Next, you will click the Make it button. With this command, the software will guide you through the entire cutting process.
7. For this project, you will insert the Premium Fine tip blade.
8. Next, stick the vinyl to the cutting Mat.
9. Install the Mat to the Cricut Maker and wait for the cutting to be done.
10. Once the cutting is done, take the vinyl sheet off the Mat and start weeding.
11. Weed out tur letters from the vinyl using the weeding tools from the Cricut Toolbox. Leave the rest of the vinyl sheet intact.
12. When you are done with weeding, take off the vinyl from the backing paper and set the vinyl sheet on the Mat where you want to place the text.

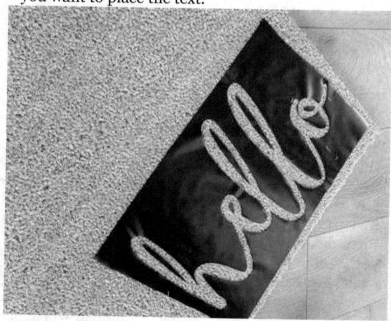

(Mat with vinyl sheet set as a stencil)

13. This will act as a stencil.
14. Now use the craft paint and the foam brush to color withing the stencil.
15. After the painting is complete, wait for a while before removing the vinyl.
16. Waiting for 10 to 15 minutes will be sufficient.
17. Now let the paint dry. It will take a while, and then your Mat is ready to use.

Decorative Birdhouse

This birdhouse project is a beautiful one. This birdhouse project is included in the free Design Space projects. This is a ready-made project with all the settings and measurements in place. You must select this project and click "Make it." But be careful; if you are a beginner, you might want to try a few more projects before you attempt this one. This is an advanced project. For this birdhouse, more than two different materials are used in the making. The base materials will be chipboard. Three different cutting tools are also used. This birdhouse can be kept for yourself as decoration. It is also ideal for gifting.

(A decorative birdhouse)

- Cricut Maker Project Level: Advanced (Competent)
- Time: Start to finish 4 hours
- Materials and Supplies:
  - Cricut Maker Machine
  - Easy Press 2 (Cricut)
  - Hooked weeding tool
  - White glue
  - Damask patterned chipboard
  - Glittered vinyl (Silver)
  - Cricut chipboard
  - Fusible fabric(red)

- premium permanent vinyl in pink and red
- Adhesive foil (red)
- Knife blade
- Fine point blade
- Rotary blade

- Instructions:
  1. For every project, it is most important to first have a clean, clutter-free space.
  2. Then collect all the materials, supplies, and all the different blades you will require.
  3. Once all of this is done, turn on your laptop or device with design space and start. As this project is already present in the Design Space, you will not have to design in this project.
  4. Just go to the projects and choose the Birdhouse Design and click 'Make It."
  5. Now as simple as it seems, to complete the whole project will take some time and expertise.
  6. When you click the Make its option, the cutting process can be started.
  7. The software will give you instructions regarding the materials and blades to be used.
  8. According to the instructions, this project will be cut into 20 mats.
  9. First, you install the Knife blade and cut the Demask Patterned chipboard as Mat one.

(Cricut maker during the cutting process)

10. Now for mats 2 and 3, you will use the chipboard. The design space will also instruct for multiple passes for compete cutting. You can follow the instruction to fully complete the cutting for each material sheet or Mat.

11. After cutting the chipboards, the blade will be changed to a fine point blade. With this blade, the three types of Sheet will be cut:

- Adhesive foil
- Premium permanent vinyl both sheets
- Glitter vinyl sheet

12. The standard cutting mat will be used for these cuttings.

(Cutting the Adhesive foil)

13. Next, the blade must be changed to the rotary blade. With these, the fusible fabric cutouts will be easily cut.
14. This step will end the cutting process. You can now put away the Cricut maker. And start weeding with the hooked weeding tool.
15. When all the wedding is done, you will start assembling the project. The instructions for that are given in the project file.
16. First, you will transfer all the vinyl cuttings appropriately to the chipboard cuttings.
17. Transfer the fusible fabric to the rooftop cuttings with the help of the Cricut Press 2. Heat the easy press to 300 degrees Fahrenheit and keep the cupboard and fabric under the press for 30 seconds. Let it cool down before use.

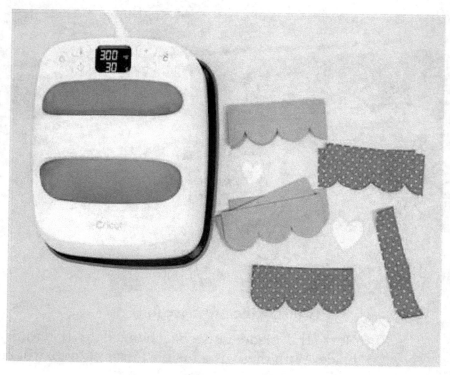

(Heating the Easy Press 2)

18. When all the projects are ready, join them together with the help of white glue.

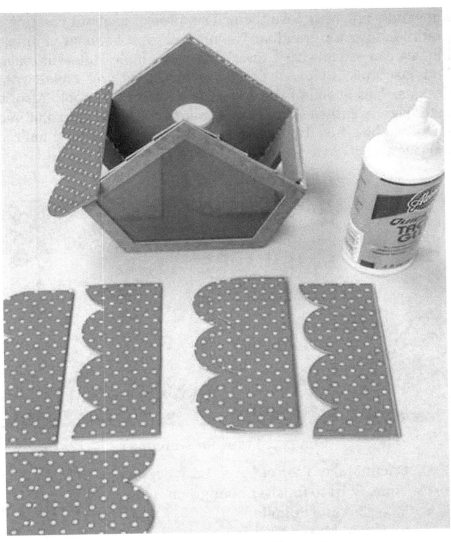

(Completing the Birdhouse)

Cricut Maker Mug for Grandpa

Grandparents are such a blessing. They are like a second set of parents, only gentler and kinder. Being with one's grandparents is always an enriching experience. Sometimes we need to let them know how much we love them. This project is about creating a gratitude mug for grandpa. The tutorial topic is about grandpa, but you can use this basic tutorial to create many different mugs. You just must follow the same instructions and create your designs. This is one of the easiest projects in this book. Also, it takes significantly less time to be completed. Also, personalized mugs can be gifted. In the previous chapter, selling personalized mugs is also given as a business idea.

(Competed Mug for Grandpa)

- Cricut Maker Project Level: Easy Beginner
- Time: Start to finish- 1 hour 30 minutes
- Materials and Supplies:
  - Cricut Maker Machine
  - Standard Grip Mat
  - Vinyl
  - Cricut Scraping tool
  - Measuring tape
  - Blank Mug (can be white or any other color)
  - Scissors
- Instructions:

1. Clear up all your working space. Turn on your laptop or device where you will design the project.
2. Collect all the materials necessary for the project.
3. Open the design space and insert the design or text you want to transfer on your mug.
4. Here we selected some text.
5. Upload your design.
6. Now, as we are creating vinyl for the mug, we need to adjust the text to be placed easily on the mug's curved surface.
7. You can even select a design from the images or make projects available in the design space. It is more fun to create your designs, though.
8. Now use the rotate option to align the text according to the mug. You can also measure the mug beforehand and size the text accordingly.

(The curve button)

9. When you are satisfied with your design, click the attach button on the right-side layers panel. This is so that all the text is cut together when cutting in the Cricut Maker.
10. Next, you unlock the design. If you do not unlock the design, you might not be able to customize it.

11. Adjust the dimensions of the design. A standard-sized mug should have a 5cm-by-5cm design that will look good.

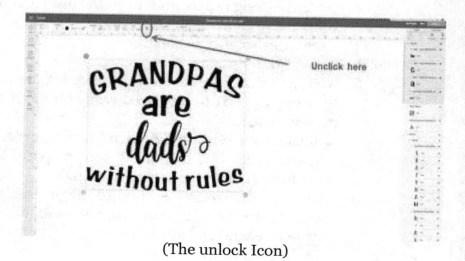

(The unlock Icon)

12. When you are satisfied with your design, click 'Make It".
13. Follow the instructions and set up the Mat and viny carefully, and let the project be cut.

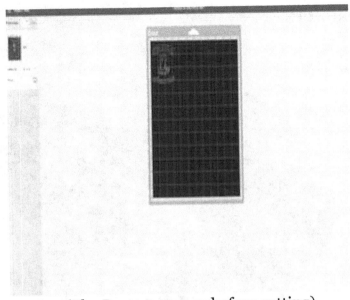

(The Prepare screen before cutting)

14. Once the project is cut, weed it with the help of weeing tools.
15. Clean your mug of any dust particles.
16. Now prepare the transfer tape of the same size as the design.
17. Please take off the backing from the transfer tape and attach it to the vinyl. Press to remove all air bubbles. You can also use a scraping tool to smooth the transfer tape.
18. Carefully remove the transfer tape with the design.
19. Now your beautiful mug is ready.

Coasters

(Colorful coasters)

Everyone roams around their house with a hot cup of tea or coffee and places it on their furniture, ruining your wooden tables and marble counters. For this purpose, we need coasters. And if you are a creative person, you would want to design and create your coasters. Cricut sells coasters in two designs, one square, and one circle. These are sold as a pack of four. The circle and square ones are slightly different. The circle ones are ceramic, and the square ones are ceramic on the top and have a cork backing. To design and create these coasters, the method is the same. In this project, we are going to design the coasters with Transfusible Ink Transfer sheets. These are a product of Cricut, these are like heat transfer sheets, but the difference is that they transfer colored Ink onto the surfaces, and the Ink is transferred to the product by applying heat. The finished products give a watercolor effect. The design space has quite a few patterns and quotes for these coasters. You can create four similar coasters or can choose four different designs from the Design Space. This project is easy to make but does involve some level of expertise, especially to transfer the Ink onto the coasters. Also, you need a bit of practice to use Easy Press 2.

Let us start this project and create some beautiful coasters.

Cricut Maker Project Level: Intermediate

- Time: Start to finish – 2 hours
- Materials and supplies
  - Cricut Maker Machine
  - Ceramic Coasters by Cricut
  - Standard grip mat
  - Infusible ink transfer sheets
  - Cricut Easypress with a heat mat
  - Fine point blade

- Instructions:
1. Clear up all the working space. Set your laptop or device. Keep all the materials near you.
2. Once you enter Design Space, you will start a new project.
3. Go to images and search for round coasters.

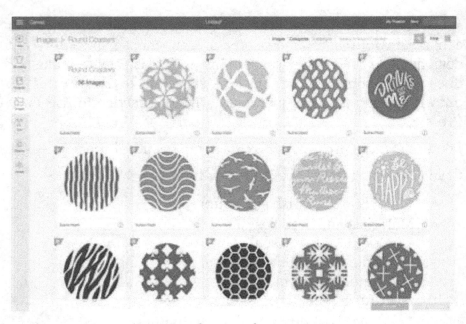

(Image selection for coasters)

4. You will get several designs in the library. If you are a beginner, it is always wise to choose pictures and projects in the Design Space. The sizes of the projects are compatible with Cricut products. In this project, we are using Cricut coasters. If you choose a project from the design space library, the sizing will be proper. However, if you want to design your project, the coasters' size is 3.5 inches by 3.5 inches.

5. After choosing the design, you can duplicate it. If you are making four coasters, you replicate the image four times and select the same color so that all coasters can be cut on the same Ink Infusible Sheet.

6. You can align the design according to your desire. Also, by alignment, you can save your infusible ink sheets.

7. Next click 'Make It.' After that, on the Prepare Screen, select the Infusible Ink Transfer Sheet as your custom material.

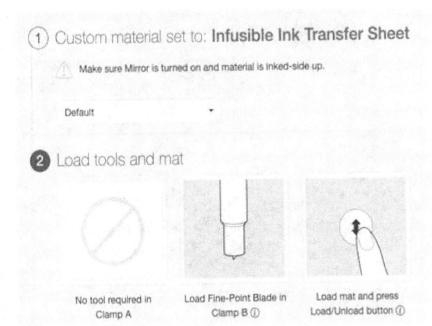

① Custom material set to: **Infusible Ink Transfer Sheet**

⚠ Make sure Mirror is turned on and material is inked-side up.

Default   ▾

② Load tools and mat

No tool required in   Load Fine-Point Blade in   Load mat and press
Clamp A   Clamp B ⓘ   Load/Unload button ⓘ

(Instructions and settings for the Infusible Ink Sheet)

8. Do not forget to mirror the design if you have text on it. If you just have a pattern on it, it will not necessarily matter. But the text must be mirrored. For some designs, to appear the same as the screen, it is best to mirror the image before cutting.

9. The blade used for these sheets is the fine point blade. Check that this blade is installed.

10. Prepare your Standard Grip Cutting Mat and the Infusible Ink Transfer sheet. The transfer sheet with liner side down on the Cutting Mat. Do not be worried if you feel that the colors appear dull on the Sheet. These colors appear very vibrant on the finished product.

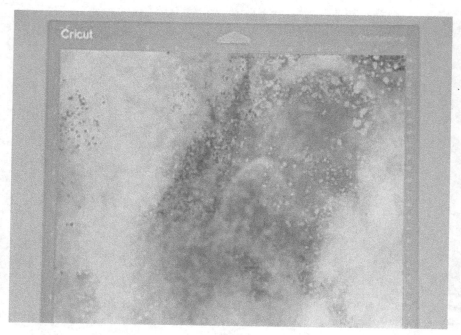

(The Infusible Ink sheet adhered to the Cutting Mat)

11. Next, the cutting of the project takes place. Insert the Mat into your machine and wait for the project to be cut.
12. Remove the Sheet from the Mat. The Infusible ink sheet has two sheets. Remove the thin Sheet. Now you will be left with the Sheet with the Ink.
13. Next, weed out all the negative space.
14. Now cut all the coaster cuttings separately.

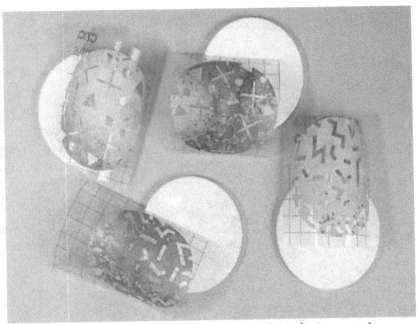

(Blank coasters and Transfusible Ink Cutouts)

15. Now prepare the Easy Press 2 for the design transfer to the coasters.
16. Follow the heat instructions on the Infusible Ink Sheet.
17. You will heat the Easy Press to 400 degrees Fahrenheit.
18. Next, you will align your design and coaster for the transfer of Ink.
19. First, place the heat mat and place plain cardstock over it so that it is not damaged. Then put the weeded design with the Ink side facing up. After that, place the coaster, the shiny side placed in the Ink sheet. Set the coaster directly on the design. Now put the butcher paper on the coaster that comes with the Ink Transfer sheet.

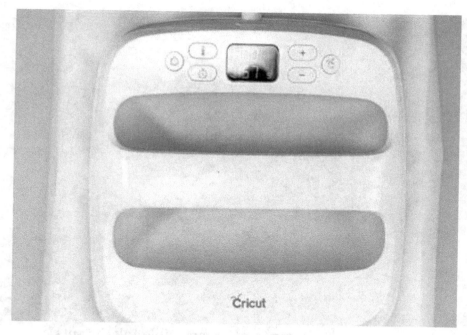

(Easy Press 2)

20. Now apply the Easy Press 2 for 4 minutes.
21. Remove the Easy Press 2 and put it on its bracket.
22. The coasters are ready but do not pick them up with your bare hands because these are too hot.
23. If you want to pick them up, use an oven mitt.
24. Do not place on wood or plastic surface; place some Sheet to place the coasters face up.
25. Your beautiful coasters are ready.

Wooden Earrings.

Jewelry is every girl's weakness. There are very few girls who do not wear jewelry or do not like jewelry. Customized jewelry is a creative way to express yourself. With the Cricut Maker, you can cut and shape several different materials. The main difference with the Cricut Explore is its ability to cut thicker and heavier materials. It would help if you had a ticker and more sturdy material to create jewelry. So, the Cricut Maker is ideal for jewelry creation. You can design all kinds of pieces, like necklaces, chunky rings, earrings, bracelets, anklets, etc., with the Cricut Maker. Personalized and handmade jewelry make for unique gifts. You can gift your loved one's pieces according to their unique personalities. And with Cricut Maker, you can create jewelry with more than 100 materials. In this tutorial, we discuss a specific pinecone earring made from wood veneer, which is wood, sliced into very thin layers and then adhered together with strong glues to make it stronger and more durable. This is an easy-to-follow step by step tutorial to create beautiful earrings.

(Pinecone Earrings)

- Cricut Maker Project Level: Intermediate
- Time: Start to finish – 2 hours
- Materials and Supplies:
  - Cricut Maker
  - Earring hooks
  - Jump rings

- Jewelry pliers
- Deep cut blade
- Cricut Wood Veneer (light brown)
- Cricut Wood Veneer (dark brown)
- Strong Grip Mat
- Cricut Scraper
- Cricut Tweezers
- Cricut Brayer

- Instructions:

1. Before starting any project, it is always best to declutter the working space. Collect all the materials required to complete the project
2. Turn on the Design Space. For this project, you will have to make a Cricut Access purchase. If you are a subscribed member, this will be available for you for free.
3. Select the Pinecone Earring Svg and pay for the design.
4. Upload the design.

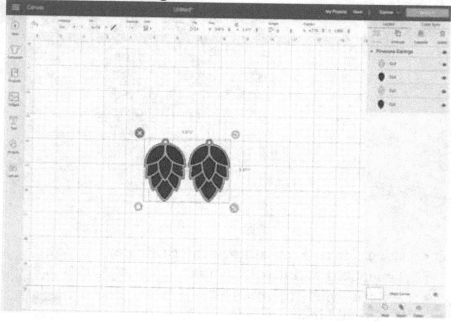

(The canvas display of Pinecone earrings)

5. A reasonable size for such earrings will be 2.5 inches tall. If you want to change the size, you can easily do it on the Edit Toolbar.
6. When you are done editing, click 'Make It.'
7. When you enter the Prepare Screen, you will see that this project will be cut on two mats. It means that this project has two layers or two parts. Do not make any changes on the Prepare screen.

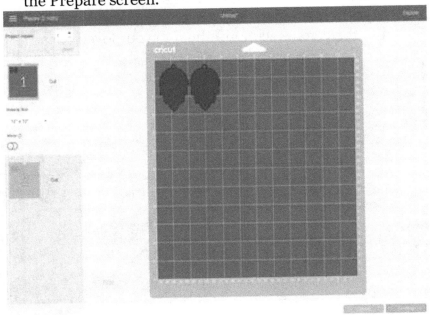

(Prepare screen)

8. On the Make screen, select your custom material to be a wood veneer.
9. Next, check the blade in your machine; it should be a deep cut blade.
10. Prepare your material. Place the veneer on the Strong Grip mat. Use a brayer for the proper adhesion. If it is needed, you can fix it with tape.
11. Now let the first layer cut.
12. Next, prepare the other Sheet to be cut in the same way.

13. When both sheets are ready, peel off the wood from the Mat.
14. Weed out the cuttings from the wood.
15. Now assemble your earrings. Align the two layers, darker at the back and lighter in the front.
16. Connect them with a jump ring and close it with the pliers. Now connect with the fishhooks, taking care that you attach the fishhook in the correct direction.
17. Your beautiful earrings are ready to wear. You can either use them yourself or gift them to your loved ones.

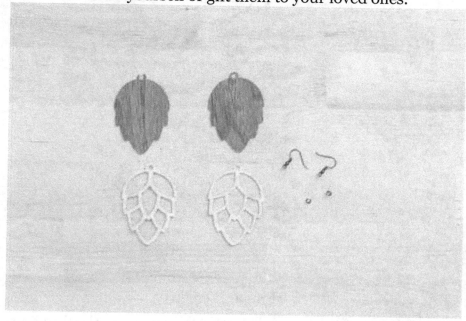

(Wood veneer cutouts)

Felt Bows

This is also a ready-made project. We will make these creative and beautiful bows together. These bows are easy and straightforward to cut as the whole project with instruction is being used. The assembly process is time-consuming and will require more concentration. During the assembly of these bows, you must be very careful. The glue will stick the bow together, and it takes a while for the fabric to fully attach with glue. If you do not work with patience, this assembly may become very messy. And messy projects do not give a good impression.

The bows you will create are usually used for decoration. You can sow or glue a felt boy to a baby hairband.

These bows can be glues to blank pins to create beautiful hair embellishments for little girls. They can even be glued to scrunchies to create decorative hair ties.

In the following project, three different styles of od bows are included. With step-by-step instructions, the project is relatively easy to follow.

(Finished Felt Bows)

- Cricut Maker Project Level: Intermediate

- Time: Start to Finish – 2 hours
- Materials and Supplies:
  - Cricut Maker
  - Rotary blade for fabric
  - Hot glue gun
  - Strong Grip Mat
  - Cricut Felt material of different colors
  - Scissors
- Instructions:

1. Clear up the working space. Turn on your laptop or device with a design space.
2. Start a new project.
3. For this project also you will need to purchase an image from Cricut Access. You will have to pay a small price if you want to buy an individual image, but it will be easy to access if you are subscribed to Cricut Access.
4. Choose the Felt Bow SVG.
5. Next, upload the template on the Design Space. It will appear on the Canvas.
6. You can now resize and change the color of each bow on the template.
7. This is ready to make the project, so remember not to unlock it. The individual bows are already attached.
8. If you want to cut the entire project with the same color and same material, you can unlock the design. Then attach all the components and cut on the same piece of felt. However, in this tutorial, we are making each bow on a separate piece of felt.
9. When you are satisfied with your design, click the 'Make It' button.
10. Next comes the Prepare screen. Each bow appears on a separate mat.
11. On the Make screen, choose the correct material. Since we are using the Cricut Felt, the Mat's size will not have to be adjusted.

12. Check that the rotary blade has been installed in the Cricut Maker. This blade is especially for fabric and is exclusive to the Cricut Maker.
13. Next, prepare the felt on the Strong Grip Mat.
14. Install the Mat into the machine and let the cutting be done.

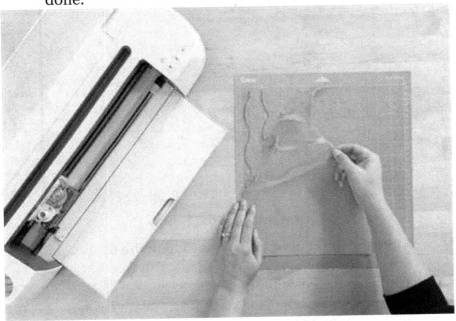

(Removing the negative area)

15. Remove the felt from the Cricut Mat. It will leave behind all the components of the bow.
16. Repeat the same procedure with other felt sheets.
17. Separate all the cut pieces for the bows.
18. Now when you have got all the cutouts, assemble the bows.

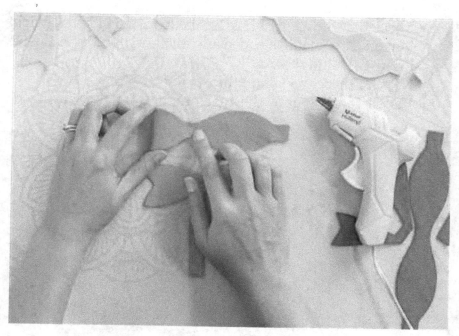

(Assembling the bows)

19. Take the first cut out, fold one side to the center, and stick it with the glue. Repeat the same with the other side. You will have the basic bow shape.
20. Turn over the bow and stick it to the larger bow cut out with the glue gun.

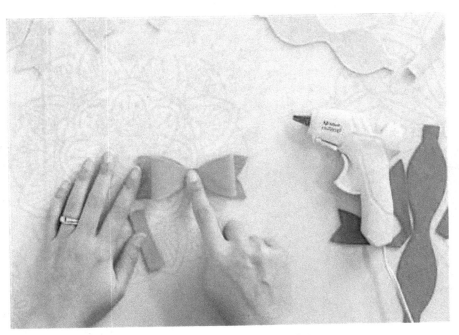

(Simple Bow Assembly)

21. Now wrap around the thin cutout in the middle tightly and secure it at the back.
22. The other bow is also assembled similarly by stacking and sticking the pieces from bigger to smaller. Then secure them with the center cutout.
23. The next bow is cut in a way that it has four corners. Each corner must be brought into the middle and glued in the center.

(Bow With four Edges)

24. Next, you will wrap around the center cutout and glue it securely. At the back, you will attach the ribbon cutout.
25. You can also mix and match these bows or can make them in solid colors.
26. These bows can be used for decorations for kids and holiday gift packaging. These bows will be most useful to glue on little girls' headbands, hairclips, and hair ties.

Baby Onesie (Everyday Iron-On)

Babies are the cutest creatures on earth. They have the tiniest hands and the most innocent faces. It is always so wonderful to create stuff for kids. It is prevalent among parents these days to make their kids wear onesies with exciting quotes and quirky designs. If you are one of those parents who enjoy following trends, then this project will interest you. In this DIY project, we will be creating a customized onesie for a baby. Whenever you are making stuff for infants and kids in general, use the right quality materials. Especially fabric. Kids have extremely sensitive skins. They cannot wear materials that are not pure. It is best to use good, quality cotton-based material for kids.

Baby onesies are a great gift idea. With the Cricut Maker, you can create personalized gifts for your loved ones. Cricut sells onesies for babies so that you can use them. They are compatible with their easy iron-on sheets. You can also use regular blank onesies for your projects. They work equally well. This project will create a baby onesie with an iron-on design created by the Cricut Maker. One thing about iron-on designs is that you always must mirror them before sending them to cut. Otherwise, the design orientation will be the opposite of what you see on screen.

With all the useful instructions in mind, let us start our baby project.

(Iron On design Onesie)

- Cricut Maker Project Level: Easy (Beginner)

- Time: Start to finish – 1 hour
- Materials and Supplies:
  - Cricut Maker
  - Cricut Onesie
  - Easy Press Mini
  - Hook weeding tool
  - Cricut Everyday Iron-on Sheet
  - Standard Grip Mat
  - Lint roller
  - Bucher paper
  - Scissors
- Instructions:
1. Clear up your working space. Collect all the materials you will require for the project. It is always less time consuming if you have a clean working space.
2. Open design space. This is a simple tutorial for a onesie. Start a new project.
3. Open the images and select a cute animal image. Upload it on the canvas. Fill it with the checkered background so that the outline of the image is cut. Adjust the size of the image.
4. Now from the text icon, add text to your design area. You can select the font, size, and style of the text.
5. Now align the text with the image. Set the proportions so that the image and text look compatible.
6. Now select the image and text and attach them with the attach button in the right panel.
7. Now adjust the size of the design.
8. As it is a baby onesie, the right size would be 3 inches in width and 4 inches in length.
9. When all is determined, the press makes it.
10. See on the prepare screen that only one Mat is shown.
11. Then on the made screen, select the Everyday Iron-on Sheet. Also, mirror the project.
12. Prepare the Cutting Mat and the iron-on Sheet.

13. Now let the project be cut.
14. When the project is cut, remove the iron-on Sheet from the Mat and cut around the design edges with scissors.
15. Now weed out the negative space with the weeding hook tool.
16. Now, prepare the blank onesie. Clear all the dirt and dust on it with the lint roller.
17. Place the design on the onesie. Align it properly.
18. Put a butcher paper on the design.
19. Turn on the Easy press mini to the recommended temperature for cotton.
20. Now iron on the design. Keep ironing for about a minute so that the design is fully transferred.
21. Your cute onesie is ready. Either you made it for your baby or created it to gift it to someone; this is one of the most satisfying projects you will ever make.

Infusible Ink T-Shirt

T-shirts are always in fashion. Sometimes you want to personalize your shirts with your creative style. Sometimes you come across such quotes or saying that you want to say out loud. What better expression would be other than wearing those quotes. Personalized T-Shirts say so much about your personality and individuality. If you are an expressive and creative person, you would surely be interested in creating your shirts. You can do this easily with a Cricut Maker and beautiful Infusible Ink Transfer Sheets. Infusible Ink Transfer sheets come in beautiful patterns and designs. There are soft and pastel-colored designs, as well as vibrant colors and patterns as well. When you see an Infusible Ink Transfer sheet, you would feel that it has dull colors. But when it transfers on materials, it has very fresh and vibrant colors.

This is a relatively easy project. But the only hurdle will be the Ink transfer part. If you are a beginner, this part can be a little difficult and messy for you. Also, another thing is handling Easy Press 2. This heats up fast and too high temperatures. Be incredibly careful while handling it. If you have children, you might want them to be out of the working area when dealing with heat.

With all these instructions, let us start making our beautiful T-Shirt.

(A fun shirt made with Cricut maker)

- Cricut Maker Project Level: Easy (Beginner)
- Time: Start to finish- 2 hours
- Materials and Supplies:

- Cricut Maker
- Easy Press 2
- Heat mat
- Light Grip Mat
- Infusible Ink transfer sheet (Shaylee pattern)
- Scissors
- Cricut Blank White T-Shirt
- Cardstock
- Butcher paper
- Lint roller
- Hook weeding tool

- Instructions:

1. Clear up your working space. Collect all the things you would require for your project.
2. Open design space. Select a new project. The design shown in the picture is available as a ready-made project by the name of the rainbow is my favorite color. You can pay a small price and select that from Images as an SVG. Or you can design your shirt as well.
3. If you want to use the same file, you buy it and then upload it. The file is of the accurate proportions for a medium-sized shirt. So, there will be no need to adjust the size and straight ahead to the Make it button.
4. But in case you want to make your design, you add some text. Edit the fonts, size of the text. You can also write text in three or four lines and change each line's font and size to make it more interesting.
5. You can add basic shapes to your design and set them around your text.
6. Or you can add an image to your design
7. After setting up your design, check the proportions and alignment, and remember to attach the text and images to print the design all in one layer.
8. When it is attached, you can determine the size of the design.

9. For a medium-sized shirt, the right size would be 6 inches by six-inch, or if it is a larger design, it can also be 6 inches by 8 inches in size.
10. When you are satisfied with your design, press make it.
11. Next, check the prepared screen that everything is on the same layer.
12. Go to the Make screen and be sure to mirror your design.
13. Choose Infusible Ink for your material.
14. Be sure to use a fine point blade.
15. Set your Mat with the infusible ink sheet. Set the Sheet according to the instructions given on the box.
16. Let the project be cut.
17. Remove the Infusible Ink Sheet from the cutting Mat.
18. With the hook tool, weed out the negative space. Be extremely careful in weeding the project.
19. Cut out the design from the Sheet.
20. Prepare the T-Shirt for the project. Clean it with a lint roller.
21. Put cardstock in the middle of the t-shirt layers. This is because the color from the Infusible Ink sheets can be transferred to the other side of the shirt and ruin the design.
22. Place the Infusible ink sheet on the t-shirt. Try to align in the center.
23. Place butcher paper on the Sheet.
24. Heat the Easy Press 2 according to the instruction for cotton material.
25. Press the design on the t-shirt for two minutes.
26. Now, wait for a while before taking out the cardstock.
27. Let the Ink dry for 3 to 5 minutes.
28. The colors appear to be very vibrant when printed on the material. Otherwise, the sheets seem to be very dull.
29. Do not worry if you feel the sheets are dull; they are highly pigmented.

Tote Bags

Another very fashionable accessory is a tote bag. You can make your style statement with cool, personalized tote bags. Tote bags with creative patterns and quotes are real in things these days. These are suitable for a nice picnic day on a beach with friends. Or you can gift your friends a nice creative tote bag with their favorite quote or their favorite-colored design. They are straightforward to make and are useful. In this project, we are going to use Heat Transfer vinyl on a tote bag. This is a simple project, and you can make it in many ways you please. You can make a customized tote bag with other materials as well Cricut has Glitter Iron On sheets for a blingy finish. If you are into bling, you should try making the tote bag with a glitter sheet. Another option to create a beautiful watercolor effect on the tote bag is to use Transfusible Ink Transfer sheets. You can also use Transfusible Ink Markers for creating beautiful designs and text for the tote bag.

This project is made, keeping in mind the people who have just started or had to purchase their very first Cricut Machine. The instructions are kept simple, and only one layer is included to avoid confusion. Once you are used to making one-layer projects with ease, you can always make more complex and detailed designs. But to gain confidence, one must first master the most basic and straightforward projects.

Let us start making this beautiful and elegant tote bag. One crucial point to always remember whenever using transfer sheets, always mirror your design before cutting. If you cut the design without mirroring, the design will be cut inverted. In some cases, this might work out okay if you only have specific patterns and designs to cut. But in the case of text, you must mirror it. This point is repeated a lot of times in this book, because this mistake occurs very commonly.

(Beautiful Tote Bag)

- Cricut Maker Project Level: Easy (Beginner)
- Time: Start to Finish – 30 minutes
- Materials and Supplies:
  - Cricut Maker
  - Easy Press 2
  - Heat Mat
  - Canvas tote bag
  - Measuring tape
  - Butcher Paper
  - Heat Transfer Vinyl (Color of your choice)

- Weeding tool
- Standard grip mat
- Cricut Fine tip blade
- Scissors
- Instructions:
1. As in all projects, the first instruction is always to clear up your working space. It is really important to keep the working space clean and clear. This makes the steps of the project to be followed smoothly.
2. Collect all the materials and supplies required for this project.
3. Turn on your device or laptop and log in to Design Space.
4. Start a new project.
5. Click the text button. Write your favorite quote or your favorite saying.
6. Now edit the size and the font of the text.
7. Arrange and align it according to your design.
8. You can also use the rotate option to slightly curve your text.
9. Be creative.
10. The most important thing for this project is sizing.
11. You should always measure the size of your tote bag.
12. The design should not be tiny; neither should it be huge.
13. It should be of an appropriate size.
14. For a medium-sized tote bag, the design size should be 4 inches by five inches in length.
15. Align the design to the leftmost corner so that the rest of the vinyl van is saved for future usage.
16. Once you have aligned and sized your text, click the Make It button.
17. See the settings on the Prepare page are correct. Then move forward.
18. Now on the made screen, first select the heat transfer vinyl.

19. Next, mirror the image. This point is critical. If you forget this step, the design will be cut in the inverted orientation. In easy words, the design will be ruined.
20. When you are satisfied with everything else, set up your cutting Mat and attach the heat transfer vinyl to the Cutting Mat.
21. Let the Cricut Maker start its work, and you wait for the creative magic to happen.
22. Once the design is cut, remove the Sheet from the cutting Mat.
23. Cut out the design from the vinyl sheet and weed out the negative space.
24. Now heat the easy press 2 according to the instructions for a canvas bag.
25. Prepare the bag by rolling on the lint roller on it.
26. Put the vinyl on the tote bag. The vinyl should be placed in the center.
27. You can determine the center of the bag by folding it in half and ironing the centerline. This way, you will get the perfect center.
28. Place the vinyl in the center of the tote bag. Cover it with butcher paper.
29. Use the Easy Press 2 to press on the design for about two minutes and then remove it.
30. Take away the butcher paper and the backing of the transfer sheet.
31. Your beautiful tote bag is ready for use.

Conclusion

So, by now, you must have come to an understanding that the Cricut Maker is the holy grail for the creative soul. This die-cut machine offers you a plethora of possibilities. You imagine, and the Cricut Maker turns your ideas into reality. The best part about this device is precision and finesse. To attain perfection is the actual goal for a crafter, and this is precisely what the Cricut Maker offers.

The most outstanding feature of the Cricut Maker has is its ability to cut and shape more than 300 materials. It ranges from the softest, most fragile materials like crepe paper to much harder materials such as wood and leather. The other feature worth highlighting is that it is the only device in the Cricut Machines range with a rotary tool that cuts fabrics with precision and without any need for backing material. Now, this feature is greatly beneficial. You have an endless opportunity with fabric. You can make quilts, fabric dolls, accessories for little kids, and whatnot. You can use your creativity to make mixed medium projects involving fabrics. Perhaps an essential feature of this model is the Adaptive Tool System. This is extremely user friendly, and most importantly, any new tools that Cricut will launch will be compatible with the Cricut Maker. So, you will only be needing the Cricut Maker for all your future creative endeavors.

Another essential part of the Cricut Maker is the software. Design Space is the software to control and create on the machine. The best part about it is that the interface is quite simple and easy to use. Just a few clicks, and you can carry on with your creations and DIYs. You can download the Design Space application on your laptop or mobile and can even use it offline. In the Design Space, you can either create your project from the very beginning or choose from various projects already included in the program. Another feature, Cricut Access, is a subscription-based service that gives you access to hundreds of thousands of pre-saved projects to choose from.

So, if you are a creative person and love to create beautiful stuff for yourself, your family, friends, or even for business, then the Cricut Maker is just for you.

Cricut Design Space

A Complete DIY guide To Learn How to Use the Best Tool to Start Cricut Projects

By Melissa Johnson

Introduction

Welcome to Cricut Design Space's comprehensive guide. Cricut is a device used for projects that are designed and cut. It offers you the ability to build various DIY designs, varying from cards the vinyl design invites and many more. No wonder what innovative concept you may have, with Cricut's help, you will possibly create it. Cricut has a free downloadable software named Cricut Design Space in order to be able to carry the designs out into the future.

Cricut Design Space is a Computer programming framework designed by the creators of the Cricut machine, Provocraft. Although the system itself makes the client, in a range of sizes, to cut numerous types and textual forms, the Cricut Design Space brings it to an undreamed level. Just attach the Cricut via a USB port to the PC, introduce the product, and unleash a completely different aspect of creativity.

The key benefit of the Cricut Design Space is the willingness of customers to weld or link letters together just to frame a solitary cut. The days of sticking each letter, in turn, are gone. Expressions of letters and shapes will currently be fastened together before cutting, making it easier and smoother to introduce cuttings to businesses than every time in modern memory. Another benefit of the Cricut Design Space is that before cutting, the shapes and letters may be managed extensively. Customers are only constrained to just adjusting the scale again, so now they will be willing to adjust the shape attributes to support their general design all the more probably. To get the exact look the crafter wants, each image may be stretched, rotated, and twisted. Although the Cricut Design Space has several advantages, the opportunity to merge pictures from multiple cartridges into one design is an undisputed top preference.

A perfect way to be a skilled crafter is to find a medium or partner that allows you the independence to pursue your passion. Cricut has created an awesome machine with advanced cutting technologies for anybody who wants to go into crafts, which can help you cut, design, and carry all your beautiful art ideas to life. To minimize your practice time and save yourself a lot of headaches, it is important to know what equipment and accessories to use for your Cricut! The Circuit machine is very flexible and can be used to assemble any project time that you can think of for many kinds of materials.

Apart from being a cutter of templates for a scrapbook, the Cricut machine has many purposes. Other items, such as wedding invitations, wall decorations, and so much more, can be created with the patterns themselves. You just have to think creatively. There are no barriers; even if there are any, they would only be a figment of your fantasy.

Chapter 1: All about Cricut

A Cricut is a cutter that helps you to cut and make stunning and gorgeous crafts from materials that you didn't realize existed. You can however draw, emboss and generate fold lines to make interactive creations, gift items, boxes, etc., based on the model you use. The Cricut cutting machine works, kind of, like a printer. You create a layout on your computer in the form of an illustration.

1.1 What is Cricut?

A Cricut is a specialized cutting device/machine that can be used to cut different materials for making crafts, projects, and much more. It cuts patterns, images, and text. Though many individuals contemplate a Cricut as the one that just cuts vinyl and card-stock, it may cut synthetic fabric, balsa wood, adhesive foil, and more. In addition to cutting, the machine has a writing and scoring connector with the Cricut machines: Explore One, Explore Air & Cricut Explore Air 2 (the latest versions offered by Cricut). A Cricut machine is common among craftsmen, party organizers, enthusiasts of DIY, and more.

The machines that have become accessible can also design with pens, compose with pens & score stuff for crisp, simple folding, in order to cut all kinds of materials.

What can a Cricut be used for?

Mentioning all will be a lengthy list- But, here's a quick list of things you can make with Cricut.

Projects for school- Cricut machines can be used for making school projects.

Card-stock projects- Designers & Event organizers can create greeting cards, event invites, and decorations for events, costume pieces, embellishments for Bible journals & much more.

Vinyl projects- For outside projects (possibly updating a mailbox) and kitchen products (such as cups) that might be washed by hands, use continuous vinyl. For fence patterns, make use of removable vinyl.

Iron-on patterns-Iron-on vinyl (often called heat transmission vinyl) is one of the most common uses for Cricut to produce personalized tops, bags, caps and much more.

Foam craft projects- For children's crafts, garlands, and more, craft foam projects are enjoyable.

Window grips projects- Think of making the window grips for vacations! With the Cricut machine, like the Preschool Design ideas, window sticking material is easily cut into various shapes and fixtures.

Cut & Print projects- The Cricut helps craftsperson to print pictures or images on their device and then cut with the Cricut in tandem with their home printer. There are several choices for personalized gifts or favoring for weddings, etc., from printer-friendly magnets to sticker paper.

Projects of faux leather - make elegant faux leather jewelry or fashion accouterments or apply a leather look to passes, cushions and more.

Projects of Adhesive Foil & Washi Sheet- For certain designs, adhesive foil & washi sheets are great. The adhesive foil brings a glossy, metallic appearance to every project.

Projects of stenciled wood - Use stencil vinyl to make your personal adhesive stencil, add it to wood & then dye. After the dye has settled, detach the stencil vinyl then there you go. Use stencil vinyl to make unique wood symbols and much more.

1.2 How Cricut Works?

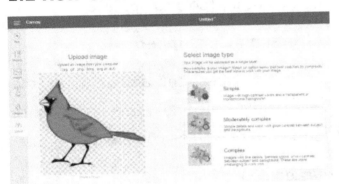

All of the Cricut machines are surely some of those machines that do amazing things. The cutting machine operates like a printer, kind of. You develop a layout in the form of a picture on your computer, then submit the image via a USB cable or a Bluetooth wireless link to the cutting machine.

There's a little computer in the machine which controls a cutting blade. It's almost about operating an inkjet printer using an ink nozzle. While the nozzle is instructed by a printer where to dump ink, the computer of the machine specifies the blade exactly when to make cuts. The same way your cutting machine operates for writing, score, engraving, or embossing.

Your template will be sent to the cutting machine & the pen is instructed what to write by the computer inside. In order to create the invention, you designed, it can also command the numerous other tools to operate.

What is the Cricut machine equipped with?

There are numerous cutter types, and among them, the things that come with each machine varies. Yet, there are certain aspects that all machines come with.

Each package comes equipped with:

- The machine for cutting
- A fine-point quality blade and blade housing
- A mat for cutting
- A USB Cable
- A power connector
- A welcome guide for easy configuration

- Free trial membership for their software

- Access to at least 25 free projects that are ready-to-make

- Materials for a project to practice.

Many versions come with more items, such as various blades, scoring wheels, or a unique pen for writing.

1.3 Why Getting a Cricut?

There are thousands of examples for using a Cricut makes crafting life easier & better. Moreover, using a Cricut enables more design than anyone else had been doing, only because it's too simple to make stuff with a Cricut! None of this is to indicate that you can't make great projects by hand if you're not using a Cricut; a lot of things might be carved out of blades or perhaps an X-Acto knife. But using Cricut and WAY more efficiently is WAY easier than doing it by hand; still, Cricut will cut materials that are much tougher than one can do with scissors.

1. Incredibly flexible. More than 300 materials can be cut by A Cricut, and more can be scored, engraved, debossed, perforated, etc. A Cricut may create a different universe of opportunities that you can't do by hand, regardless of what type of crafting is involved, Do-It-Yourself (DIY) crafts, or interests you have.

2. It is reliable. A Cricut not only do lots of various tasks. However, it fixes them far more easily than you might ever do with the help of your hands. By effectively spacing the patterns it cuts on the material, it can preserve your energy, save you from tingling hands, and may also end up saving supplies and money.

3. it's smart to use. Although the machine could sound a little complicated at first, once you're comfortable with the fundamentals of the machine, it's quite simple to use.

4. To create cool things, you don't need to become a designer. While evaluating whether a Cricut becomes worthy for you, your specific design abilities are probably not a concern. You may create your own photos and graphics for your machine to use, but you can also produce hundreds of already designed pictures, graphics, & projects.

5. The Cricut devices are reliable and high-quality. The devices are well-built and made of quality components that do not ever tend to fray or split.

6. Cricut's machines are "long term." The Cricut Maker will use a lot of different blades and equipment for the latest Adaptive Tool System, and Cricut is still designing the latest tools for the maker. Each new kind of tool or blade brings a whole new range of outcomes for crafting, accessing the same device you have already! (Sadly, this latest equipment is not integrated with the Explore machines, but the Cricut Explore devices are also completely worth it because if you do not have to be trained to sculpt, deboss, perforate, etc. for the device, they will save you some money.)

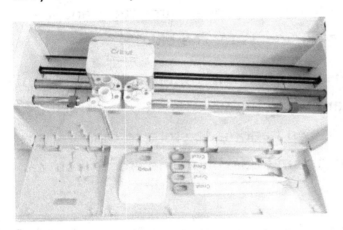

Who can use a Cricut?

Anybody can use a Cricut; it does not make a difference whether you are tech-savvy or not. The only thing that is really "necessary" to use a Cricut is wanting to manage things! If you think you're a craftsperson, DIY person, hobbyist, maker or some other kind of person who likes to create things with their own two hands, it's certainly worth buying a Cricut since you're going to have a lot of use out of it!

- **Cricut equipment is perfect for teachers;** you can use Cricut to make art sheets, school projects, holiday decorations, and loads of other fun things for your classroom.

- **For weddings, Cricut machines are excellent;** you can use them to create cake toppers, wedding invitations, name tags, and loads of other arrangements for the big day.

- **For owners of handmade stores,** Cricut machines are fantastic; you may use them on Etsy or that your own handmade store to manufacture or customize hundreds of online items you can offer.

- The Cricut machines are amazing for any form of the maker.

- If you are a crafter who has pain, muscle spasms, or some other kind of thing that affects your hands, a Cricut may be an amazing device.

Who cannot use a Cricut?

While nearly anyone can take benefit from using a Cricut, However, there are certain individuals that might not be worth a Cricut.

- If you like hand - made products, but you choose to purchase these on (ETSY) instead of creating them by your hands, a Cricut may not be for you. You're obviously not going to utilize a Cricut often to make it viable if you'd rather hire somebody else to create it rather than creating it yourself.

- While you love to do stuff, but you're super busy, and you're not really finishing the projects you're beginning, a Cricut might not be for you.

A Cricut may not be for you while you are an irregular crafter or enthusiast. It's actually not worth the expense if you just utilize the Cricut device either once or twice within a year. It's definitely not worth it, though you have an upcoming celebration or even you're a teacher. While you don't think you're going to use the Cricut device/machine either once or-twice a year.

Chapter 2: Cricut Model's Overview

Provo Craft and Novelty, Inc. developed the Cricut machines. The location of Provo Craft is in Utah. The business is fifteen years old yet was founded on December 21, 2003.

2.1 Old Cricut Machine Models

There were very solid old Cricut machines, plenty of buttons, recycled cartridges, and took very tiny cutting area. We should be glad that we have devices like Cricut Explore Air 2 and Maker today, but it might be a lot of fun to glance back at the past. Card makers and scrapbookers were genuinely targeted by inventive machines. Electronic cutting devices, at least within home craftsmen, were fairly novel and offered a better mode to do it all oneself from home. Currently, anything from creating vinyl decals & iron-on transfers to cloth & sewing designs and cutting cork or other forms of heat transfer is used by Cricut machines.

Following are the older Cricut machine models.

1. Original Cricut Machine

Although it might not be attractive, the device that initiated it all was the Cricut Personal. Cricut cartridges had been used by this device, and a computer wasn't required for it to operate.

It was a very trivial device/machine, with a rather tiny space for cutting. It was unable to render extremely complicated cuts, nor was it able to complete projects greater than 5.4 x 12 inches. The width of the cutting mat was just six inches broad, so it was just a simple handicraft machine used for cutting

2. Cricut Create

The next machine created by Cricut is the Cricut Create was (also normally recognized as Provo Craft back in the time). The Cricut Create machine was just a similar design as the 1st Cricut machine, although a few improvements were made. Compared to the 1st machine, it devises a completely new look and has the newest shades. It also enhanced the monitor panel. Technology and layout features were both expanded, and an eight-way rotating blade also came with it.

3. Cricut Expression

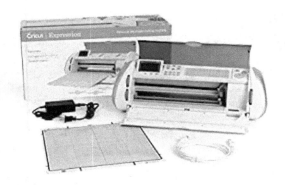

Next came the Cricut Expression, bringing some more substantive improvements. Most importantly, this was the 1st Cricut with a cutting capacity of 13 x 26 inches, and the minor cuts were better. A broader variety of materials could be sliced by Expression 1, including heavier products such as poster board & vellum.

It was still possible to use this machine individually without a machine, but the program for device use was certainly improving. Cricut Craft Room was the predecessor to Cricut Design Space, and the program was incomplete usage for the Expression.

4. Cricut Expression 2

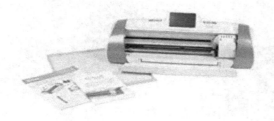

A very famous machine in its time was the Cricut Expression 2. The machine's manner had changed; it came with a bigger, quicker, full-hued screen that made things much simpler. There were many wonderful features and enhancements to this machine, like:

- 1500+ designs already-loaded (text styles, pictures, quotes, etc.)

- Improved designs for manipulation-resizing, spinning, turning, mirroring.

- For more photos, use the Cricut Craft Room.

Cricut was progressively fetching more renowned and more famous among crafters by the time Expression 2 came out.

5. Cricut Imagine

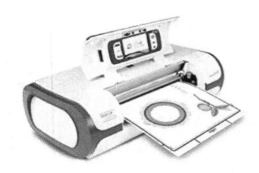

The Cricut Imagine machine is special since it is the sole machine that can print as well as cut. It was a printer & cutter by Cricut. In addition to the Imagine, to print and cut, you just ought to get a curvature cutting machine.

Ink for Cricut Imagine: Cricut partnered with HP to create a specially formulated black and three-colored ink to fit with the Envision. Unluckily, at the moment, the system was not the most successful for consumers, and it endured discontinued very soon, while Cricut tried developing machines that were more aligned with the real one.

6. Cricut Mini

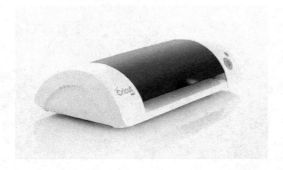

The Cricut Mini cutting machine, you don't need to be mistaken with the Cricut Easy Press Mini, was just another little personal cutter. It was the 1st machine that required a computer to be used, with a narrower cutting range of 8.6 inches. While it wasn't as great a success as the Cricut Expression collection, this machine was marketed as a smoother, more portable, and simpler machine to move.

7. Cricut Cake

The Cricut Cake device remained part of the Martha Stewart Collection of Cricut Cake Machines. Actually, this device was used to decorate cakes, cookies and cupcakes. It could amend filo dough, sheets of frosting, gum paste, and much more.

2.2 Current Cricut Machine Models

With Cricut's brilliant collection of automated electronic cutting machines, all the anticipation, stress, and anxiety are stripped out of crafting, and you are ready to get creative and live the dream as the machine handles all the arduous bits for you. There are 3 Cricut devices for today's crafters to choose from. What is the Cricut Device, and what is the best one? In a nutshell, Cricut's devices are here.

The Cricut Maker, which deals with intense materials such as wood, leather & thinner metal and also more paper-friendly ones such as vinyl, cardstock and vellum, is the most flexible Cricut device, opening up a vast world of crating, with possibilities for draping and engraving, as well as cloth cutting. For craftsmen who prefer paper craft and card production, or vinyl-cutting designs, the Explore Air 2 machines are a strong match since they have the same roles as the Maker in these places, and both machines can accommodate cuts of up to 12 inches deep. The latest Cricut Joy is the beginner level crafting device, perfect for daily card making and label making, but this gorgeous Cricut machine has nothing ordinary! Its higher cutting width is 5.6 inches, but it can cut without a cutting mat, unlike the other two machines, utilizing a Smart Materials roll for long cuts of approximately 19 feet.

1. Cricut joy

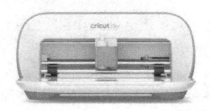

The Cricut Joy is a tiny, lighter edition at 5'' x 8'' and less than 4 lbs. (introduced February 12, 2020-accessible March 2020). In the Cricut product line, The Joy adds two additional features not found elsewhere. The Joy is capable of cutting specific designs up to 4 feet long and frequent cuts up to 20 feet with advanced accessories and fabrics (labeled Smart Materialists).

Features

- Only Cricut device which can cut utilizing Smarter Materials without the need for a mat

- Tiny and portable for quick day-to-day crafts

- Using the complete Smart Materials roll, you can cut patterns approximately 21 feet lengthy.

- To cut amazing paper-cut cards for about 5.5 x7.25 in, use the inventive Enclosure Card mat with the already-scored card packs.

- Ideal for newbies to Cricut

Advantages

- The lowest cost rate of the three Cricut Smart Cutting Machines

- Best if you don't have ample space

- Easy and simple to configure

- Great for daily vinyl cards and labels

- Insertion of Card Mat & Card Packs ensures that a card that is bought from some shop would never be used again

Disadvantages

The minimum variety of products being cut by the least regulated machine.

- The pens for Cricut and equipment meant for the Maker and Explored Air 2 can't be used. Yet you have an additional Cricut device; you may require distinctive pens for Joy.

- The range of cut patterns is limited to 5.6" around.

- The mat which comes with the device only works on 4.3 x 6.6-inch products. There are wider mats that people might randomly purchase,

- The device only has a solo lock, so you can need to change tools if you'd like to both write and cut on the very same task.

What it'll cut?

Cricut Joy could cut about fifty materials, including acrylic, iron-on, cardstock, peel & gooey label paper, sticky foil, luxury paper, plastic chalkboard, sticker paper, sheet, iron-on, flat canvas, foil paper, shimmer cardstock, regular cardstock, swirl vinyl, Infusible Ink transmission papers, cardstock, acrylic, Smart Vinyl, Crafty Iron-On, window cling.

2. Cricut Maker

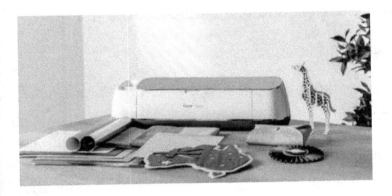

(Released August 20, 2017) With the Design Space, which is cloud-based, downloadable software, the Cricut Maker machine is used. It does not operate optimally. An internet link is needed when accessing Design Space on a desktop or laptop computer. You can use the offline functionality of that software by using the Design Space app on an iOS device (iPad/iPhone) to use your device and Design Space without an internet link. The Cricut Maker is a flexible machine with adjustable cutting and scoring heads.

Features

- The Maker is the device for you if you want the chance to develop the equipment and tools at your hands while your art skills grow.

- This is the Cricut series' most effective cutting machine; this can cut materials around 2.4 millimeters thick and gives up to 4 kg of power.

Advantages

- The Maker has all the functionality of Explore Air 2 and much more.

- The device comes with a revolving blade that enables the cutting of almost any material and the cutting of delicate papers like tissue paper.

- It has a comfortable pattern to stand up the tablet or phone while utilizing the Design Space software from one of these.

- Built-in storage gives you a convenient place to store tools and equipment in the body and parts of the device.

- When you have one, you would never wish to craft without it,

Disadvantages

- You would need to buy extra tools to maximize the usage of the Maker's more advanced features, such as engraving, rupturing, and forceful cutting.

- This is the maximum costly machine since it is the top-spec.

- It is the weightiest and biggest machine since it has to exert 4 k of cutting capacity.

- Without it, you will never wish to craft till you have one,

What it'll cut?

Cricut Maker will cut approximately 300 items, such as leather, acetate, plastic, balsa, bamboo linen, basswood, boucle, denim, broadcloth, burlap, calico, silk, cardstock, suede, Chantilly lace, sequins, duct tape tubes, copy paper, polystyrene foam, linen, art foam, crepe paper, tulle, double knit, pants, EVA foam, cotton, synthetic fur, synthetic brogues, felt, flannel, simple fabrics, etc.

3. Explore Air 2 by Cricut

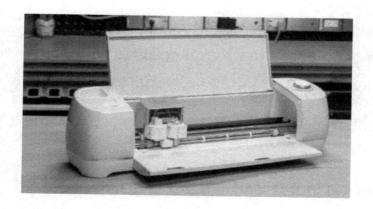

It cuts two times faster, a minor update from the Air. It comes in a number of shades and functions with the latest application for Circuit Design Space.

Features

- Quick Cut mode, which is ideal for designs that generate mass

- Cuts an extensive variety of products up to a thickness of 2mm

- The Shrewd Chooser material segment dial is simple to use and helps you to visually see if the machine is fixed to the right material

- You get a dazzling Yellow, Green Mint, or Multi Blue Cricut device with colorful models.

- Lightweight still fine design.

Advantages

- It will cut up to 11 x 22 inches of vinyl and decals that make it perfect for patterns that cover wide places, such as the facade of t-shirts and window glasses.

- For a short and simple finish, the machine can cut & score complicated present box layouts.

- There are two clamps in the machine. However, two separate tools may be used at a similar time.

- Incorporated storage offers you a convenient place to put tools and accessories in the frame and sections of the device.

Disadvantages

- There's a really loud Quick Cut feature. Use the normal cutting pace for a softer cut.

- It cannot cut very fragile items, such as tissue paper,

- A tool named scoring stylus must be purchased separately.

- Massive machine with a footprint that is just marginally minor than The Maker, but can cut with fewer materials

What it'll cut?

Around 100 products such as paper, acrylic, iron-on, cardstock, adhesive labels, foil, bamboo, canvas, sticker paper, art foam, cork, duct tape panels, thin synthetic leather, felt, plain cardboard, soft chipboard, shimmer paper, wax paper, washi paper, wrapping paper, plastic wrap, parchment, fused fabric & window cling can be cut by Cricut Explore Air 2.

4. Explore One by Cricut

★★★★★ 307

Related to the other Explore machines, but with just a single holder for the tool. You can cut and compose, but in two steps, you have to do so.

Features

- Great starter machine at an incredible cost

- Cut, compose, and a score of 100 materials

- Sharp-Point Blade for a broad variety of common craft products for cutting

- Compatible with Deep-Point Blade, Scoring Stylus, and other tools (sold separately)

- Software Design Space® for iOS, Android, Windows®, and Mac®

- Free uploading of your own photos and fonts

- Compatible with cartridges by Cricut

What it'll cut?

Cricut Explore One is an easy-to-learn and simple-to-use digital cutting machine for DIY projects & crafts. One hundred materials, like cardstock, vinyl, and iron-on, to cut, compose, and score. This inexpensive machine makes it simple to fulfill your artistic idea, from cards to personalized T-shirts to home décor. The on-the-go interface on your laptop, smartphone, or iPhone. With thousands of pictures, fonts, and ready-to-make designs, browse and play. Or develop a layout of your own from scratch.

5. Cricut Explore

Each has a double tool holder for the Cricut Explore, Explore Air, and Explore Air 2 so that you can cut & write (or cut & score) in 1 phase. There is a single tool holder for the Explore One, so it can cut & write (or cut & score) in 2 stages.

Explore Air & Explore Air 2 have built-in Bluetooth, so you would need a Cricut Wireless Bluetooth Adapter to use it with your mobile iOS or Android smartphone or to cut wirelessly from your phone to Explore One and Explore

6. Cricut Air Explore

This is a wireless gadget that can cut paper and more into cloth. It works with the existing application of Circuit Design Space.

Chapter 3: Cricut Design Space

Cricut Design Space is the design app from Cricut that helps you to cut with the Cricut Maker & Cricut Explore machines.   The oldest software classified as Cricut Craft Room has been used by older machines such as Cricut Expression 2 and Cricut Mini. Design Space is a Mac or PC device downloadable app that helps you to make original designs and import ready - made designs, or to use them free of charge or to buy designs specifically into Design Space. Even on your Android or iOS smartphone you can use the Design Space Software, although it does have more functionality limitations. If you do have an older machine cartridge, you may connect it to your Design Space account and then use the cartridge with your newer Cricut machine. The Cricut Explore has a slot for cartridges so you can bind your cartridges a bit more conveniently. After you have connected your cartridges to any device registered with you, you might use your design in Design Space

3.1 What is Cricut Design Space?

Design Space is software from Cricut that can be downloaded to your Windows computer for free. On the program, you will find prepared layouts which you can cut with the machine immediately, or you can upload pictures, fonts (or including your own!) of Cricut to create something more unique. Around 75,000 pictures, 400 fonts, and more than 800 predesigned Make it now designs are lodged in Cricut Design Space. The projects for Make It Now is already completed for you, and all you have to do is click on "Go."

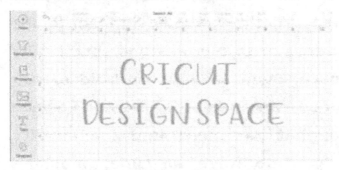

How can you get Design space?

In order to download the software to your computer, go to design.cricut.com. You can make an account after its downloaded and start using it instantly.

Is Cricut Design Space free of cost?

You can download the software for free, and you can discover some available Cricut fonts & photos to use right away. In the Design Space, you can even use your own device's fonts and upload image files into the program to be used. You may pay a small charge to use specific

Cricut images & fonts or pay a recurring fee for Cricut Use, which requires you to use Design Space's wide catalog of images and fonts.

There are several characteristics; it's challenging to know where to begin.

Home Screen

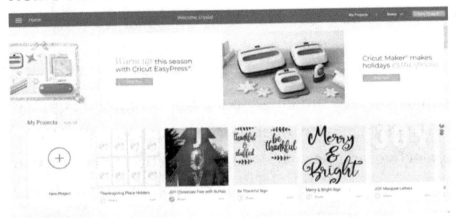

When you start the Cricut Design Space, it's the first window you can see.

On the top left (that's the menu), you'll see 3 rows accompanying "Home," then "Welcome, then "My Projects.

Afterward, you can pick the Cricut Machine Form from the drop-down board (whether in Cricut Maker/Cricut Explore Family), then finally the icon "New Project."

Cricut advertisements are preceded by (at the top of the main screen) My Projects (projects that are all retained),

Cricut Access (ventures that you may purchase a paid plan or use with the Cricut Access affiliation), professionally prepared Projects (projects produced by talented designers), most famous Video Seminars, and finally some rows of ideas for seasonal projects. Let's have a view of the topmost left corner of the "Three Lines" menu bar.

Open/View Profile

You may update the line "About Me," profile image and access you're publicly available projects here. All of these are elective and not necessary to practice Cricut Design Space (however useful if you choose to make shared projects with someone else)

Home Screen

It takes you directly to the key screen.

The Canvas

Take you to the canvas, the core portion of the design space that you're going to use.

A little farther down, you'll see all the info on your canvas.

New Machine Configuration

If you have a brand new, unopened Cricut Maker, Cricut Explore, or Cricut Easy Press 2 machine, this is the point to set it up, configure, or upgrade it.

Calibrating

Calibration choices for the Revolving Blade, fine Blade (knife), & Printing Then Cut can be found here.

Managing Specific Materials

Here you can notice all the substantial adjustments you have attached to the machine.

The Term, Cut Weight, Several-Cut, and Blade Style settings may be adjusted for every sort of material.

You may even select a new material if you're clicking the whole ways to the end of the screen.

Firmware Upgrade

That really seems to be where you actually go to modify the wired machine firmware you've got.

It's a brilliant idea to monitor this timely.

Details of accounts

You can access information about your accounts here, such as account settings, payment configurations & affiliation data.

Connection of Cartridges

You will connect up these here while having some Cricut cartridges. This can be done only on a laptop, MacBook or desktop.

Cricut Access

You may log in to Cricut Access and track your subscription here. It's much better than purchasing particular items, plus there are too many pictures, fonts, and designs from which to choose.

Setups

You may adjust the settings of the grid of Design Space here and move the measuring units between Metric and Imperial.

Legal

You would press here to give a read to the entire Cricut machine the "fine print."

Latest functionalities

Here more details on new features can be found.

Country

You may change the country here. Australia, the UK, as well as the US are among the choices.

About Help

This leads you to Support Hub, where FAQs, tips, repair, fix, and more can be found.

Signing Out

You will log out of your account of Design Space here.

Reviews

Clicking here opens up a page where suggestions and comments may be left. Now that Home Screen, as well as the menu at left, has been protected, it is ready to be in the mince and bones of the Design Space: Canvas.

The Canvas

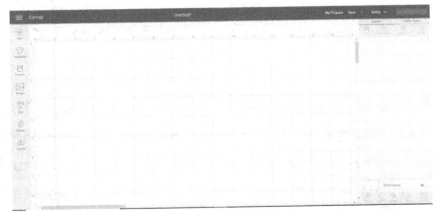

That's the workshop for your Cricut for creating things. You'll see this screen the most. It includes a wide glided work zone with top functions, a left-hand menu, and the right-hand Layers & Pigment Sync Palettes.

Let's look in-depth at each portion.

Canvas: Menu on the Left

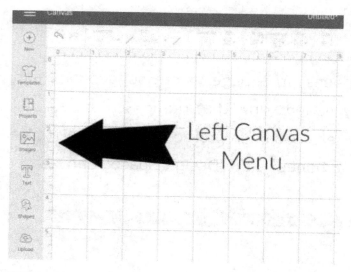

New

To begin with, a new canvas, click New. Make sure to backup it before you make a fresh canvas if you're doing work on a layout that you need to hold. If you like to conserve, Design Space may query you until it dissipates it off.

Patterns/Templates

There are predesigned models that can be used with your project to ensure that the projects are the required size. Tons are available to pick from.

You will choose various choices after you have selected a design. Also, you can change the template hue to anything you want.

Adjust template color

Click the prototype stratum at the end of the palette of layers to remove the template, and then click the erase icon.

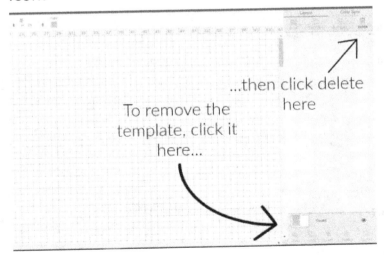

In the design space, delete a prototype. The low-profile, lightweight Bright Pad makes it easy to craft while lowering eye pressure.

The Projects

Here each of the already prepared designs specified in the Design Space and those you have uploaded can be found.

Drop-down Projects menu of Design Space Pictures

You'll notice all the photos accessible in Design place under Photographs (and there's a Ton of them).

A number of the photos are provided with an Access membership of Circuit. "On the upper left, they have a green button, "a." And also, for those that are free for all, there is a handful that you do need to order.

You can select Categories appearing on top, and it takes you to the Featured Categories screen ("Free the Week" right now, "Most Common," and "Newly Added"). In Design Space, picture categories, you'll see common types like "Birthday," Anniversary," as well as "fall" below that. You'll discover categories with labels like Martha Stewart, Disney and Marvel if you scroll down beyond that.

If you're pressing 'Filter' on the top right of the search bar, you may filter photos by property (My images, posted, free, Cricut Entry, and purchased), form (3D objects, context & borders, textures, envelopes and cards, photos, sentences, and printable), as well as layers (multi-layer, single layer).

Cartridges are next to the Groups. You will find collections of pictures there, all of which go together.

The Design Space menu for cartridges

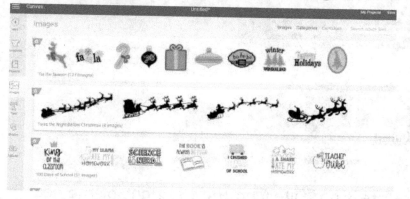

To connect it to the canvas, just press the picture and then clunk Attach Photos. Next to the cartridges, there is even a explore bar. Type in something you're searching for, and you're going to catch some fantastic choices to apply to your theme.

Text

Text Tool

To apply the text to the canvas, click here. You may use a range of fonts that you can buy (most of which are included along with access to Cricut) and use fonts that you have imported on the desktop.

Shapes

You can place simple shapes like rectangles, circles, squares, polygons, stars etc., on the canvas here. It's also where you might find score marks, which you can position with a Scoring stylus or scoring wheels on your photos to use. If there are some pieces to fold in your idea, that's where you'd like to position a score mark.

Uploading

This is where you do it if you devour any SVG and PNG image file to add to your project. Click Insert Picture and scan your device for a photo, and then click the Upload icon. Name the picture format, apply tags, and press the save icon.

Image Name and Tag - Design Space

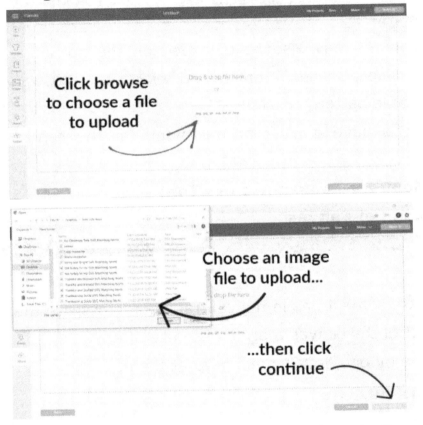

Pick the imported file to attach the picture to the canvas and select Upload Photos.

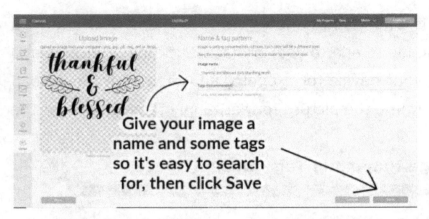

Give your image a
name and some tags
so it's easy to search
for, then click Save

A Design Fill may also be uploaded on the uploading screen. Select Upload Template and select your .jpg, .gif, or .bmp file pattern or picture.

Now, let's have a peek at the menu for the central canvas.

Key Menu for Canvas (Across Top)
Top Menu of Canvas

There are some items in the central menu crosswise the topmost of the canvas that you can use often.

Now one by one, let's have a peek at them.

Line-typing

With numerous fine point blades, guides, and pens, the Line-type drop-down menu has many choices to use.

Cut, Break

The Good Point, Intense Cut, Knife (Cricut machine - Maker), Gyratory (Cricut Maker), & Fused Cloth blades are used to cut fabrics.

Draw

With each of the Cricut pens, draw on the materials.

Scoring

Using single or even duple scoring wheels (Cricut Maker) or Stylus for scoring to score materials.

Engraving

The Inscription Tip engraves materials. (Only at Cricut Maker)

Deboss

Deboss the supplies/materials with Debossing Tip. (Only at Cricut Maker)

Wave

Using the curly edge blade to carve a curly edge pattern onto fabrics. (Only at Cricut Maker)

Perf

The Perforation Blade enables perforated surfaces to be quickly broken off. (Only at Cricut Maker)

Material Menu Color

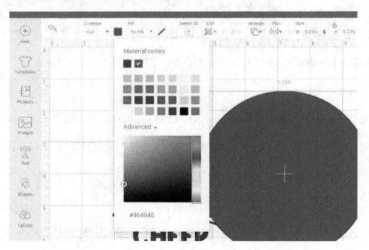

Here, you may adjust the picture layer's hue to fit the material you are going to use.

Zero or no Fill

Pick zero-fill while you just want the supplies being cut, and with Print Then Cut, no fill hue shades, or design would be added. To cut layers, that's the default mode.

Printing

If you select to use the Print, Then Cut feature, pick it. Below, you'll see the two choices.

Color

Before cutting, choose the color you would like to copy on the photo.

Design

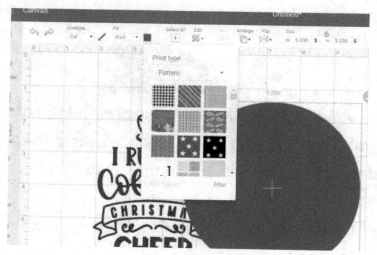

Until cutting, pick a design you'd want to facsimile on the picture. After selecting a template, in the lower-left portion of the main toolbar, you can tap Edit Pattern to amend the dimension and position.

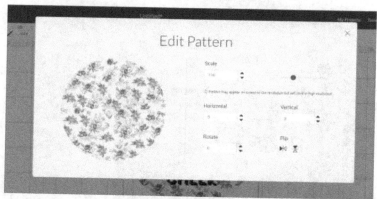

Edit Screen Pattern Space Design

Choose All

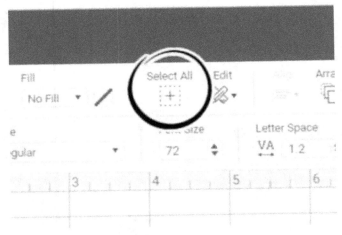

All of the stratums/layers on the canvas are picked. Click on the button once more to unselect anything if you gobble chosen something.

Editing

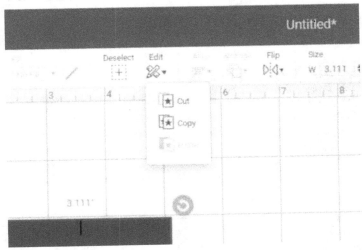

Cut: Cut a photo from canvas

Copy: On a canvas, copy a picture

Paste: Paste on canvas the cut or derivative picture

Set or Align

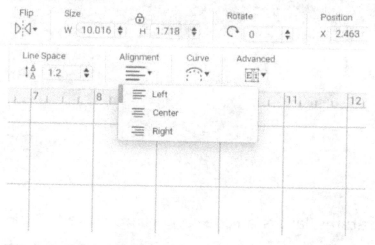

You may press this to dispose of them in various ways when you have two or even more icons selected. If you have several images picked, this menu often helps you to divide these vertically or horizontally.

Arranging

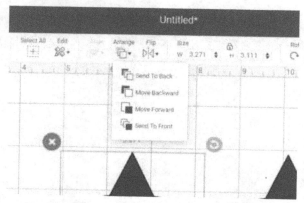

Shift to back: Shift to the rear, the selected picture.

Move Backward: Move one layer back, the selected picture.

Move Forward: Move one layer forward, the selected image.

Shift to Front: Move towards the front, the certain image you have selected.

Flip

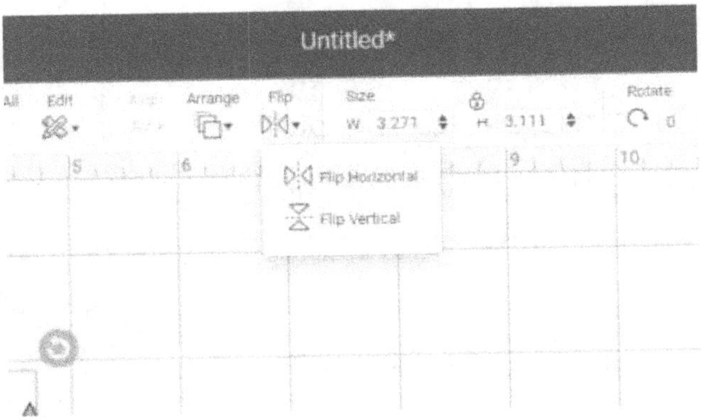

Horizontal Flip: Flip a picture from left towards right.

Vertical Flip: Flip the picture from the top pointing towards the end.

Magnitude

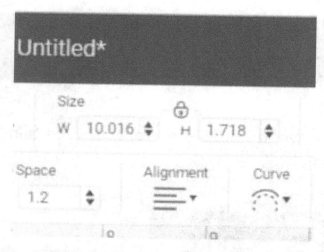

W (Width): Configure the size of the picture

H (Height): Configure the altitude of the image.

Choose the lock symbol to change the display size of the file (like whether you want to adjust the height, or conversely, but maintain the diameter the same).

Rotating

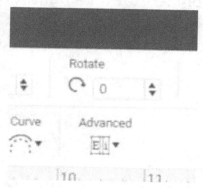

Rotate your picture to whatever range of degrees you like.

Spot/position

Position

X 2.463 ⬍ Y 6.445 ⬍

X-axis: Parallel spot

Y-axis: perpendicular spot

You likely won't use this function regularly, but for whatever reason, if you import a picture and it's off-screen, you can adjust the X & Y to nil so that you don't have to scroll to plaid it.

Writing/Texting Menu

The textual menu remains underneath the menu bar at the uppermost corner.

The fonts

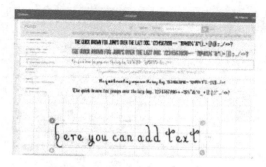

Tap the Downward Arrow button here, and the font styles menu will appear.

It is necessary to classify "All" (Machine & Cricut fonts), "System" (System fonts of the laptop), and "Cricut" (Paid & free fonts are accessible on Design Space by Cricut. Most of them would be included with your membership if you do have Cricut Access.)

Searching Bar

You can enter the font here and check by name if you know all the details of the font style that you are searching for.

Filter

You will filter The Fonts (this includes your computer fonts and your account fonts if you are a user of Cricut Access), Multi-Layer (fonts with far more than one layer to be ripped), Sole Layer (fonts with one layer to be ripped) also Writing (fonts with one sheet to be cut) (fonts that are a single line and will work with Cricut Pens or the Engraving or Debossing tool).

Styles

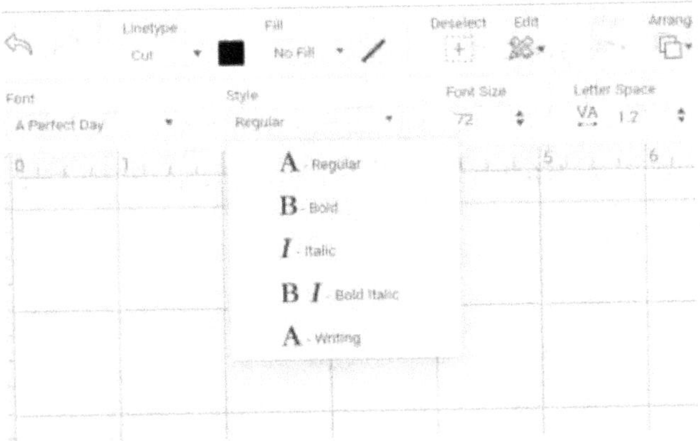

To pick a text grace, press the Downward Arrow here. You may see only a couple of these choices, based on the font you have chosen.

Regular: The default edition

Bold: Thick style

Italic: Distorted edition

Bold Italic: Sturdier and skewed version

Writing: Edition of Single Line (impeccable for Pens used by the Cricut, Etching Tip & Debossing Trick)

Reading Italic: The skewed edition of a single line (also perfect for Cricut Pens, Engraving Trick, and Debossing Trick)

Size of Font

Make the text greater or minor.

Another alternative: The size of the box can also be adjusted by pressing and moving a dual blue arrow in the lower right-hand corner.

Letter Space

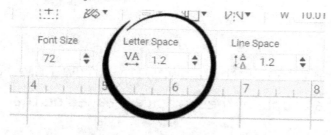

Adjust the level of space that the letters have between them.

Another alternative: you may also activate the letters & push these where you like them if you can't quite get it correctly.

Line Space

The sum of space among the lines of the text can be changed here.

Other alternatives: You can even activate text lines if you can't get it exactly perfect, then you can push them wherever you want.

Alignments

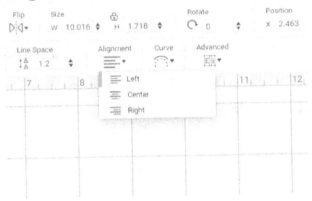

To adjust the text orientation to Left, Middle, or Right Centered, press the Downward Arrow here.

Curve

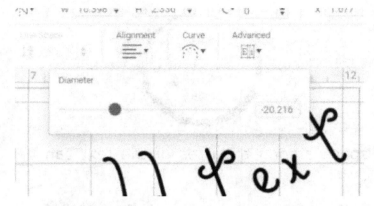

To bend the text in round or up, use this method. Move the knob to the left: The text's margins are formed upwards.

Move the knob towards the right side: the edges of the written material would be curved downwards. Even in the box, you can insert a particular number. Negative values position the edges upwards, and the edges downwards are angled by positive numbers.

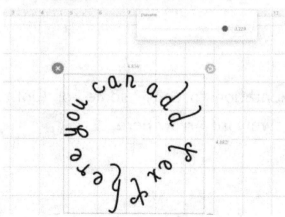

Note: The written material can be shaped into a circle if you move the knob the whole way to the left or right margin.

Design Space Curve Tool

Advanced ones

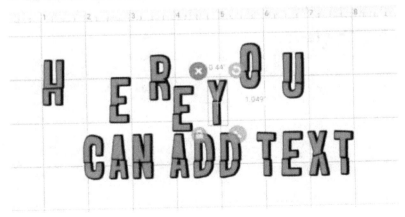

For various text ungrouping choices, press the Down Arrow button that you may utilize to adjust the placement of the text and categorically modify the appearance.

Deselect words

This released the characters so you may independently move them.

For template fonts, this choice is a necessity. Mostly with Letter Space adjuster, you can somewhat adjust the space, but to catch the slashes/lines to link, it typically also takes some tweaking.

Ungroup Lines

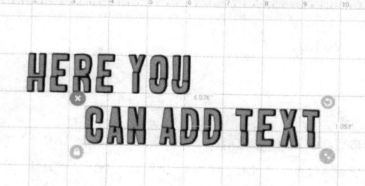

This released text lines but leaves the letters clustered together in - line such that the gap between texts lines can be changed however you wish.

Ungrouping the layers

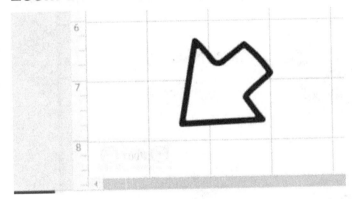

HERE YOU
CAN ADD TEXT

Whether you have chosen a miscellaneous font, it releases the layers/sheets; thus, they could be individually transferred, changed, or removed.

Zoom In & Out

There are minus and plus buttons on the lower-left crook of the panel canvas that you might custom to zoom in and out of the project.

LAYERS

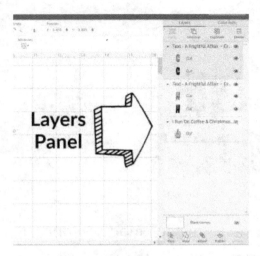

You can see the stratums of the project here. Each element of the project has a layer of its own. You can control each sheet in numerous ways by using the Layers/Sheets menu.

Let's have a little better expression at each method from the Layers Panel.

Menu with Top Layers

Group

Using this method to link your project photos, text, & layers around so you may shift or scale them quickly. In Design Space, they only stay clustered on canvas, and once you submit these to be trimmed, they can detach on the required color-based mat.

Ungroup

Using it to ungroup whatever is clustered together.

Duplicates

To create a replica of a certain layer, press this icon.

Delete

To erase the chosen layer, press here.

Menu for Bottom Layers

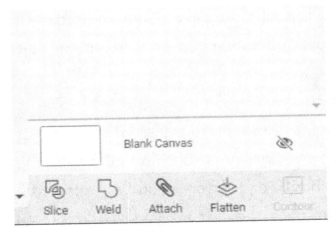

Cut

Slicing two overlapping forms into different pieces. You can cut a form obtainable of the other shape and use this by sawing parts off with the other shape to crop shapes. This option is only possible if you've picked two layers.

Weld

Merge three or more shapes that intersect or move structured into one narrative format. In edict to construct a consistent outline with Weld, it is necessary to touch the pieces.

There's not an UnWeld button at this point. Clicking on "Undo" might be the only option to unwind shapes.

While you weld a chunk of the project, thus start working on it and reminisce that you want to unweld; after soldering, you will have to remove all the work you did.

Weld is a quite useful tool, and you're likely to practice it a bunch; just ensure that while you do this, you're able to constrain

Connect/Attach

The Attach tool joins three or more stuff together or maintains them on the Cricut mat used for cutting in the same specific position. For starters, you can apply the written sheet/layer onto the picture you would like to have some written material on it in the design by using Cricut pens. Also, if there are score lines for your project, you would like to connect these to the side of the venture that you need to score.

Unlike the group, connect retains the parts and also the canvas on the Cricut mat (used for cutting) around. You may go posterior and even remove the bits if you need to, something you can't do for Weld.

Flatten

This tool connects together or holds two or more items in the same REL Flatten for printing and cutting; this attribute can be used. This transforms every photo into a file that can be accessed. If you're attempting to print a layered template, flatten it first, combining several layers into a single sheet that can be printed on the printer and afterward cut with Cricut. There is no unflatten key; however, if you want to go back, you'll have to press 'Delete' to change and redo the colors or theme.

The Contour

You may "switch on" or "switch off" portions of a picture using this tool. Pick the file, press Contour, & a window opens up whither you may individually select each section of the picture to erase it. You could go away and bring these back on if you change your opinion. This allows it to delete a portion of a pattern you don't want. Contour can work only if ungrouped is the picture you chose. If the picture would be welded or cut after that, you're not going to allow to switch the initial pieces back off or on, only an FYI.

Sync of Color

You will match the layers' colors here so that you use fewer materials.

If you have double purple layers as well as an orange layer, for example, and you want to shift one of the purple sheets to orange, you could go to the Color Synchronization menu and simply move it downwards to the layer you prefer.

Mat Preview Screen "Make It"

Copies of Project

Without needing to switch to the canvas, apply more versions of your designs to your mats. Adjust the amount to the desired quantity and press Apply.

Mats

There could be one or more mats to remove, based on how many colors the project has. They are listed in the direction in which they go, and next to them, it tells whether the photo is going to be drawn, cut, and scored, respectively.

Size of Material

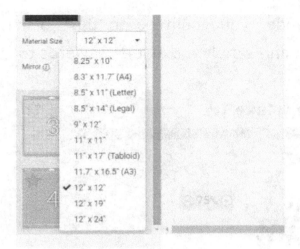

You may adjust the size of the material for the mat here. To pick from, there are many choices. Also, you can adjust the size settings here if you have an 11-22 inch mat. Design Space may ask you whether you are using an 11 x 22-inch mat or whether you want to move back and adjust your image if your picture reaches the 11 x 11-inch mat dimension.

Here, you can also transfer the pictures around on the mat. Just press the photo and slog it onto your mat where you want it to be. Until you cut it, make sure you have the material positioned at the correct point on the mat.

Menu of Three Dots

You could even select Move to some other mat or Hide Selected if you click on the three dots in the upper left corner of the image on the mat.

You may select Switch to some other mat or Hide Specified if you press the three dots in the upper left corner of the picture on the mat.

Switch to a new mat

This transfers the photo to one of the mats & changes the similar shade.

Hide selected choices

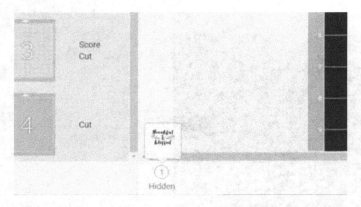

This will mask the photo from the mat so that it will not be cut. At the end of the page, an icon appears that you can press to mask the image.

Summary

You may practice all you have learned here and use it in numerous ways with your incredible Cricut machine to create some seriously cool stuff.

3.2 How to Upload Pdf Sewing Patterns In The Cricut Design Space?

The 1st thing to keep in mind is that a PDF template cannot be exported directly to the Design Space, so you need to transform the pattern into a compatible image-type format. Don't worry; it's simple to do this.

First of all, open the PDF file in the Acrobat Reader that you want to import. In the upper toolbar, click the 'More Tools' icon and then choose' Fit on One Whole Page'-this adjusts the picture to fit the screen and render it ready for conversion.

Then select and 'zip' the screen area covering the pattern piece as well as its square test/sizing. Click the Windows symbol plus Shift Key plus S concurrently to pull up the template snip feature and, using your cursor, cut out the design piece image along with the test/size square box and SAVE IT as a .jpg or .png file with your now complete page pattern image on the screen before you. (As an aside, you can always print your design out and follow the directions for downloading the paper patters below if you find this section a little confusing

Do this for all relevant pieces, ensure that every piece has a size test square next to it since this is important to accurately size the pattern piece until it has been uploaded in Design Space. Activate Cricut Design Space now and pick a 'New Project' to open the blank canvas screen.

From the project toolbar, press 'Upload.'

To view your freshly saved .jpg or .png pattern images, click on 'Upload Picture' and then 'Browse.' If the file has been recovered by Design Space, save it as a 'Complex' image, as this helps you to wipe up and delete any places you don't need, as well as maintain the lines sharp.

Using the 'Select & Erase' feature, you need to remove all places that are not a member of the pattern piece; then, your final picture is only the pattern section and the size square.

Click 'Continue'. The option to save the file as a 'print then cut file' or as a basic 'cut image' is then given to you. In particular, the arrow that tells the position in which the template should be cut from the fabric (e.g., considering the direction of your fabric's grain or greatest stretch).

Upload it into the blank project canvas until saved.

As you'll see, the upload pattern piece is a bit small-sized to the dimension of the Design Space canvas; here's where the sizing box steps in.

So, you have to adjust the file now. The most precise approach to do this is to build a square (using the shapes box in the leftmost toolbar) of the same size/scale as the measuring box of the pattern parts, e.g., it should be 1.5" here. Now resize your pattern picture (by clicking on the pattern piece and choosing the resizing tab at the bottom right) and drag before the sizing box 'grows' enough to precisely and effectively overlay the square, like this... (Remember that at this point, your sizing box & your pattern piece are related, because if you increase the size of one, you're raising the size of the other automatically.

If you intend to make sure that you have them the exact same size, Zoom in then.

Tada! Now your pattern piece must be measured properly. Next, we just need to move it so that the grain-line of the pattern parts is moving in the right course.

There are only a couple of basic steps left to take first. Otherwise, your Cricut would try to take those out of your expensive fabric, too; it is better to get rid of such test/sizing squares! At this point, the sizing box & your pattern piece are still connected as one image; you need to separate them now. Upturn the size of the red box first and use it to fully overlay the size box to 'strip' it out (using the 'Slice' feature) before removing all of them.

Now that your template pieces are a) correctly shaped, b) positioned in the correct direction, and c) the measuring boxes have been eliminated, we need to turn the pattern piece into some kind of basic cut file (Know that it originally held as a Print & Cut file to see the grain-line key)

Looking at the 1st chosen picture, you will find that the type of line is 'Cut', and 'Print' is the fill image. Select the Fill alternative and adjust it to 'No Fill'; this transforms the pattern piece to a basic cut file automatically; if handled properly, it will 'grey out.'

Finally, one really the last thing! Adjust all the template parts you cut out of the same cloth to one tone.

AND you are done. Select 'Make It' now and get the Cricut to cut your pattern out for you.

3.3 How to Upload A Paper Sewing Pattern To Design Space?

The method of importing a paper pattern is almost precisely the same as uploading your transformed PDF pattern files; you only need to bring the paper pattern files first onto your computer-for this, you would need access to a scanner if you don't have one installed, visit your local library as they are probably to have one.

Cut out the bits of paper template, parting an mm or 2 of paper along the pattern line as they have to be clearly visible to work correctly with this! Then cut out in the same fashion across the test square.

Place the pattern piece on the skimming plate, face down, and place your square size box next to it and scan it into the system (preferably one pattern piece at a time). Scan in and proceed ahead.

To save your .jpg file, press 'Save As,' rename your file, and select the ultimate folder.

Now you can continue uploading to Cricut Design Space from the 5th step in the above PDF tutorial.

The 'Images' tab,' Shapes, & 'Upload' are the three separate positions you can add designs on your mat. Images are the place where you can find everything the Cricut offers. Free pictures are accessible, and premium images are accessible and are included in Cricut Access (a subscription service). For specific photos of festive holidays (like the train for this party). Shapes are convenient, so you don't have to select a lot. There will be two separate options when you select 'Upload.' There's [a cut image] and Template Fill to upload.

IMPORT SVG PICTURES TO DESIGN SPACE

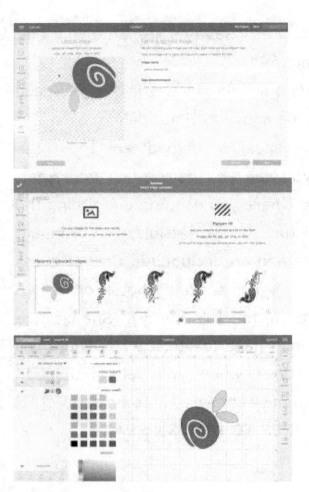

The simplest form of an image to upload in Design Space is SVG Photos. This is usually what you might buy if you accessed a 'Cut' file (like our Fresh Cut SVG Bundles). SVG refers to Versatile Vector Graphic, and that ensures that without compromising quality, you can size it up or down. Within the Design Space App, these photos still have the most modification choices, and that is because it integrates each cut as a separate item. Bear in mind

208

that it would appear even more daunting in the layers tab if you upload a larger file because there is a layer created for each cut.

To upload every file type, use the up arrow to enter the little cloud icon. Click the [cut file] upload button and pick your file. This will open up the display where you might name and apply keywords to your file. Then you should click Insert Picture, and your canvas would be placed into it. It would look like one piece when you tap on the layout and move it around. After all, everything holds together. But note that each piece is a separate layer now in the layers tab on the right? You may change each piece's color and break it off with contrasting maps. Hit MAKE IT (top right) when you've adjusted it to your liking and see how the items spread out on the mat.

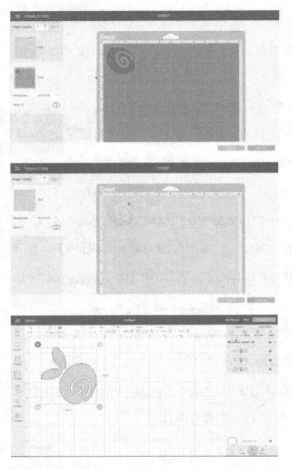

They're on mats individually. They are, of course, since they are of distinct colors because you need two contrasting vinyl colors. You'll actually go back to render all the pieces one hue and try again if you're anything like me. But the style is all muddled, you'll find. Here's the reason. By organizing all the various parts for you on your mat, Cricut Design Space aims to allow the most use of every other bit of vinyl. This could save vinyl, but if you tried to keep it lined up by hand, it could be a pain in hand. Go back to the canvas and choose all the design pieces. By bringing down (Control, CTRL) on the keyboard and clicking all the layers on the layer screen, you can do this, or you can just click and move your cursor over the layout to select all. Then, at the base of the layer board, press the little Attach (paper clip) button (highlighted in blue). This would keep the whole piece intact without destroying the separate data completely. You can see that the template keeps together this way when you click 'make it.' And because they're only linked, you can split them and adjust the size of one piece at any time or opt to remove the purple rose and the green leaves.

IMPORT PNG Photos TO DESIGN SPACE

With Cricut, PNG files are the most used ones. PNG refers to Portable Network Graphic, a lossless file format for image segmentation. It implies that it has a lot more details than a JPG (for instance), and the *biggest* part is that it can provide a clear context that makes it very easy to import and use for cutting. This is the sort of file used for Cricut MOST frequently. The images are uploaded as ONE layer, ensuring they can stay together and cut just as they are imported. What is that supposed to mean? When imported, you cannot conveniently adjust the color of one section of the design or reorganize the letters of a design.

You tap the little 'Upload' with the cloud again to upload a PNG with a translucent background, and you'll have a couple more measures than you did with the PNG. You will be asked to choose if it is a simple, moderately complicated, or complex picture after selecting your file. Then you'll be taken to a page where any sections you don't like can be erased. You should skip over this stage for a file that already has a translucent background & no pieces you don't really like. You would then be asked to select either print and cut for your Upload or just an image cut only. Choose to cut only, and your template will be loaded into the picture gallery you have submitted and can be inserted on your canvas.

You will see that it has a translucent backdrop until it's on the canvas; you can switch it around and resize it much like the SVG, except you'll find in the layer panel there's only one layer. This ensures that you can't just pick the light-bulb and print it on a new mat in a different color (although you might repeat it and draw the lines to distinguish the pieces. You'll find it when you press 'Make It' because it's all on one layer, the bits don't bounce around. It will cut everything in the same layout in which you uploaded it, making it simple to add the transfer tape and pop it on your surface.

IMPORT JPG Photos TO DESIGN SPACE

JPG is a type of photographic file named after the group named the file type. It's great for pictures as it effortlessly treats all the colors, but it can't have a translucent background. This implies that while you are importing the picture into the Design Space software, you need to adjust.

You'll note that it's not all black and transparent (because it's a JPG); it has some brightness. To make it easier to remove. This is what you're going to want to do to make things easy to get a quick range for a photo to print and then cut. If you run in Procreate, you can even do a PNG with the white background and send it without the grey background. But it's the very same moves as you try to upload it in. You may need to do a little more in this tab, depending on your picture, before going on. You can select either print then cut or a cut only picture when you move to the next page. You will see how smooth the cut lines are on the picture only cut-how that's you realize in the previous tab you don't have much special to delete.

So, in your uploaded pictures, it will populate, and you may insert it on your canvas.

Like a PNG, you'll note that there's just one layer in the layers tab. Instead of the layer-cut symbol, you can see a printer instead. It will load into its own print when you press 'Make it' then cut mat (mat with a black sensor box around it). You'd print it from here and then cut it.

HOW TO USE JPG PHOTOS FOR FILL PATTERNS (TWO WAYS)?

You'd take precisely the same measures as the above JPG picture (without erasing the background). When you embed it, apply the shape that you want the pattern to fill in. Exactly where you want the pattern to fill, place your shape over your design. When you are done, you can resize the pattern and switch it around as well. Then, by retaining CTRL on the keyboard and clicking all layers on the layer panel, click all layers OR you can either press and drag your cursor over the template and shape to choose both of them. Then, at the bottom of the layer page, click 'Slice.' This will provide you with three layers. In addition to the layers you don't want to use (or just remove them), you can press the little eye so that you are left with your pattern-filled form.

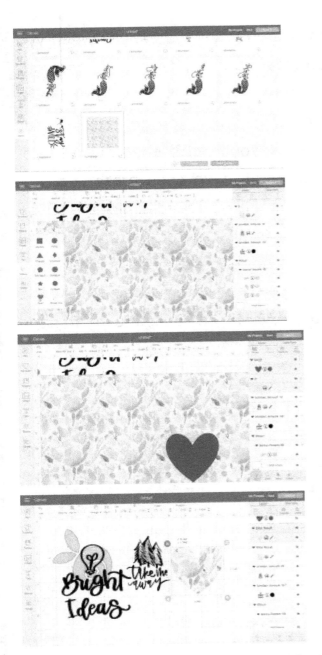

Uploading your watercolor floral (design) as a Pattern Fill rather than under the default Upload is the other option you can get this effect. You have two options when you go to the upload tab (that little cloud). You choose your pattern, and then, before you save it, you can have to name or title your pattern. When you go back to your gallery of posted pictures, you'll notice that it isn't there. That's because the patterns have been preserved, not the pictures. In the layers tab, you need to pick the shape or picture that you want to fill with the pattern first and then transform it into a print (not just a cut). Then, in the layers tab, you can see the 'Patterns' choice, and the pattern will pop up there. It will be applied to your shape when you pick it.

3.4 What is Access by Cricut?

Cricut Access is a Massive library that will help you choose and create designs that have already been designed. If you're just getting started, this is really useful. You can have exclusive fonts, icons, 3D projects if you have Cricut Access, and depending on the project you have, and if you can think about anything, you have it. For any occasion and any products, you want to work with, they have been designed. This is pretty impressive. Cricut Access is a premium subscription that allows you immediate access to an enormous archive of over 90,000 images, millions of fonts, and projects ready to be cut. You can get other perks, such as discounts on approved images, fonts, and interactive items, based on the package you have.

Font Subscription

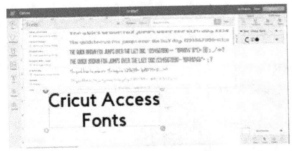

The Cricut Access - Fonts subscription is the first one. Cricut contains over 400 fonts, and whether paid yearly (in a lump sum) or $6.99 a month if billed,

This subscription costs as little as $4.99 a month.

Standard Subscription

The Cricut Access - Standard is the next tier. You can browse 400+ fonts and also 30,000+ images and cut files with this subscription. In addition, this package gives a 10 percent discount, with certain exclusions, on pictures and fonts not included in the subscription, and also on product purchases.

It is also mandatory to pay this subscription monthly or yearly. Normal memberships commence yearly at $7.99 a month or weekly at $9.99 per month. On this package, yearly subscribers save $24.

Premium Subscription

The Cricut Access - Premium is the final tier (and best overall value). The Premium membership is just that, Premium! It covers all fonts, all photos but still has a half-off discount for pictures and text aren't included in the subscription. (Exclusions are applicable) But, wait, there's more, on cricut.com, Cricut Access - Paid customers even get free Economy delivery on purchases above $50. This level of membership provides the most accessible and is the better offer overall. This is a yearly-only purchase for just under $120.

You should sign up for Cricut Membership here if you are prepared to delve into infinite amounts of awesome templates and designs. Just sign up with your ID for Cricut.

3.5 Cricut Cartridges

Cricut cartridges are collections of photos and fonts that, like Thanksgiving, the seaside, or springtime, are linked by a theme. Each picture collection may include hundreds of images, styles, or projects and ends up costing between five to thirty bucks.

The cartridges were plastic for the early Cricut machines: physical storage units that you required to insert into the cutting machine to use. You can now link these cartridges or picture sets to your Cricut ID and access them through Cricut Design Space (Explore series) or Cricut Craft Room online (Expression series). You can also buy automated cartridges without caring about trying to interact with those plastic cartridges, getting access to collections of photos digitally.

For the different Cricut Explore models or the Cricut Maker, Praise Cricut, cartridges are no longer needed. The initial Cricut cutter as well as the Cricut Expression series have been developed to be used as standalone devices with actual data cartridges, which do not need a laptop or internet access. With the free Cricut Craft Room computer design software, the Expression machines may be included, but you are still restricted to photos purchased via Cricut cartridges.

There are no cartridges necessary for any of the cutter models typically available by Cricut. Well, if you have a Cricut Explore or a Cricut Builder, and you don't ever want to imagine about a cartridge ever, you're free to go on.

All the outdated cartridges can certainly be used for some of the Cricut electronic machines. Legacy (no longer marketed by Cricut) devices, such as the Expression collection, will be using the cartridges as they still do, through manually putting them into the system and utilizing the keyboard extension, or by attaching them to the device to edit the Cricut Craft Room.

Whatever cartridges you have bought from Cricut can still be used by the newer devices, the Cricut Explore collection, and the Cricut Manufacturer. You have to connect them to the Cricut account first, however, so you can connect them online via Cricut Design Space.

How to Use Cricut Cartridges for Explore Air 2?

They must be connected to the Cricut account in order to utilize cartridges with Cricut Explore Air 2 so that you can use them digitally with Design Space.

(Warning: you may only connect a Cricut cartridge to a specific Cricut account. It is Permanent to link a cartridge: you cannot remove it, and you cannot switch it to another account. Before connecting the cartridges, please make sure that you are signed into the correct Cricut account!)

1. Go on to cricut.com/design, then, on a Windows or Mac device, login into Cricut Design Space. The cartridges cannot be connected via phone or tablet applications.

2. Making sure the Cricut Explore is attached to your computer and switched on.

3. In the upper left corner, press the menu button (it seems like a hamburger: three horizontal bars) and choose 'Connect Cartridges,' around halfway down the menu. The specification for 'Link Cartridges' is outlined in Cricut Design Space.

4. From the drop-down screen, pick the Cricut device.

5. Insert the cartridge into the position on the left-hand side of the Explore cutter, just above 'Open' tab, when prompted. The Cricut cartridge on a Cricut Explore is put into the slot.

The green "Link Cartridge" button will light up after Design Space has identified the cartridge. To link to your cartridge, press the icon.

Design Space can verify "Cartridge linked" as the cartridge is connected to your Cricut account. You will either begin to connect the remainder of your cartridges, access your cartridges, or click the X in the upper right corner to exit the cartridge link dialogue and switch to Cricut Design Space.

IN CRICUT DESIGN SPACE, HOW CAN YOU FIND YOUR CARTRIDGES?

Access to your attached cartridges & purchased photos in the Cricut Design Space is simple.

1. Click the 'Pictures' button on the left-hand menu bar in the open canvas in Design Space to open the Images screen.

2. You'll see three clickable terms around the top: Image Type Cartridges. Select 'Cartridges' to see a chart of all usable Cricut cartridges.

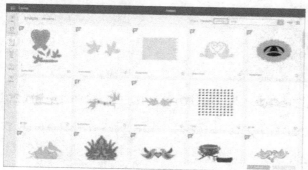

3. In Cricut Design Space, in the top right corner, "Cartridges" being selected. If you just choose to display the cartridges that you currently possess, click on the "Filter" button at the top right of the Photos window and choose "My cartridges." This would contain all cartridges that are free and bought.

4. In Cricut Design Space, a filtering option is chosen for the cartridges. If you have bought or posted individual photos, remember to check out the Pictures tab as well.

WHAT'S THE CONTRAST BETWEEN CARTRIDGES THAT ARE PHYSICAL & DIGITAL?

Physical cartridges include theme collections of photographs that are loaded onto the cutting machine physically. You will actually use physical cartridges for the Cricut Expression by loading them into the computer and picking and editing the pictures using the keyboard. This physical cartridge may also be connected to your Cricut account utilizing Design Space or Craft Room. When related, the online editing software allows you to quickly view digital copies of the cartridges. You can also hold the physical cartridge, however, or at least snap a pair of front and back images. If you ever have difficulty accessing and need to resync your connected cartridges, Cricut help can ask for these images as evidence that you own the cartridges.

Digital cartridges are thematic collections of pictures purchased digitally and are accessible through Cricut Design Space immediately. They don't have a physical aspect because nothing is going to be sent to you, and you don't need to plug it into the Cricut cutter. While you're linked to the internet and logging into Cricut Design Space, you can use them for all the new Cricut machines.

The Pros

For an inexperienced crafter, cartridges are a fantasy. It can be awesome to make your original designs from scratch, but often it's a little daunting to look at a blank canvas & wonder where to start. You can quickly find motivation with cartridges at hand, divided by every holiday or theme you can think up. Without wasting ages fussing about the template, cartridges are a simple and convenient way to plunge into making DIY vinyl decals & greeting cards.

You can find lots of step-by-step instructions for creating cartridge projects. When you're first practicing how to use a Cricut, these are awesome to use. When you start off, there are too many different topics to learn. Guides make it easier by cutting out all the conjecture. The photographs are deliberately chosen and well-curated in each cartridge. Many creative designers have spent lots of time and money only for you to use in making cartridges! You should be assured that the photos and fonts would be of good quality and function with your Cricut smoothly.

The Cricut Cartridge Collection includes nearly 600 cartridges! There are numerous photographs and projects in each cartridge that can be modified and mixed with various artistic characteristics, offering an exceptional variety of designs. You will still find something which looks perfect with any project you make. There are just too many shapes, designs, and fonts to pick from.

In fact, cartridges are of great importance. You may create hundreds of numerous designs from the core images from only a single cartridge. If you feel that your stock of Cricut cartridges has become too expensive, spend more time playing with the cartridges that you already have, and make use of that innovative value.

It would be great to have a tangible set of Cricut cartridges to find motivation for your next project. You should keep off the internet and search through a large library with your cartridge set instead of trying to gaze through pictures on a screen to locate anything to create.

The Cons

The biggest downside of the cartridge system before the Cricut Explore collection was that you were restricted to what appeared on the cartridges. With the newest Cricut devices, as cartridges are now fully optional, this is no more a drawback! You can still share your own drawings or use SVGs that you find online for free.

One big problem is that you can only connect cartridges to a single account with Cricut. If you are received cartridges or purchase some from e-bay or a thrift store, they can already be connected to someone else's account! It is indefinite to connect cartridges, and you can't switch whose account they are connected to. So, make sure you don't get fooled into getting cartridges that your computer can't really use.

You may feel like you are trapped into the Cricut brand, or perhaps even with a specific machine, after purchasing a bunch of cartridges. For Cricut, this is good, but not so nice for exchanging with the crafting and DIY groups. You can't freely swap your ideas with other individuals if you work with cartridges, one of my favorite aspects of designing new ventures! They can be conveniently exchanged with others and incorporated into the design software for other cutter products, such as Silhouette Workshop, if you use regular old 'SVG files instead.

For each Cricut unit, cartridges don't function the same. You can use cartridges even without internet in the Expressions. For the Cricut Explore Air 2, the cartridge must be connected to your account. And there isn't even a cartridge space in the Cricut Maker! If you want to use photos with a Maker from all your existing cartridges, you'll have to buy Cricut's specific Cartridge Adapter to connect them.

Chapter 4: Cricut Tools and Accessories

4.1 Cricut Accessories You Must Have

1. CRICUT TOOLS (SPECIFICALLY WEEDING TOOL & SCRAPER TOOL)

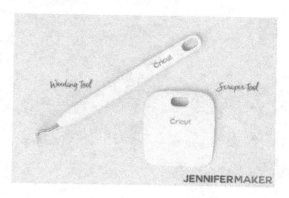

Some simple tools, particularly a weeding accessory & a scraper, are very helpful. You're almost definitely going to want to have a weeding apparatus if you cut Vinyl to extract all the pieces of the Vinyl you don't want to shift to the venture/project. Besides, a scraper is really handy while cutting the paper, as it involves a little while to pick all the tiny jiffs of paper from your mat. You can just get the weeding tool used by Cricut and the scraper apparatus used by Cricut on amazon, so having a Cricut Simple Tool Package on Amazon is a great offer. You'll even notice these devices stocked in the largest craft shops.

Weeding tool

If you want to get a single, most important tool, it's a weeding tool. The weeding tool is utterly necessary for lifting Vinyl, although the spatula and tweezers are good. There are very few different instruments that people use for weeding, and all of them work to remove Vinyl from the backing sheet.

Some other common weeding tools used are:

Pin Pen- On the smallest bits, this tool works great and will pop the vinyl bubbles without tearing as well. While it is comfortable and smooth, it does not twist when peeling to help keep down the Vinyl.

Dental Picks-Users who use dental picks stand by them for weeding. They are great, but maybe the handles are not as convenient.

Exacto knife-To gets into the subtle details; the sharp point is small and reliable enough. To be extra cautious not to damage the project, pair this with tweezers.

2. CRICUT INTEND DEEP-CUT BLADE OR CRICUT KNIFE BLADE (MAKER & EXPLORE)

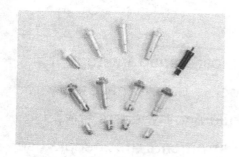

You should cut thicker materials with the Profound Blade (Explore as well as Maker) and the Knife Blade (just for Maker). If you bought a specific bundle, including it, none of these would come with your Cricut.

If you really want thicker materials to be cut, depending on the machine, you would require either or one or both of the blades.

3. CRICUT SCORING STYLUS/SCORING TOOL

To get acquainted with Cricut accessories, the scoring stylus & scoring kit are all you want. In reality, one of the best things a new Cricut owner needs a scoring system (for Cricut Explore machine) or a scoring accessory (for Cricut Maker owners).

Notice that owners of Cricut Maker can also use the scoring stylus if they wish, but you will receive a better score from the scoring tool. With the help of a scoring gadget, you may create a greater range of paper crafts. It is a simple paper crafting product that creates a huge contrast. Remember that if you're not trying to do paper crafting, you do not require this accessory.

4. Ball of Aluminum FOIL

An aluminum foil ball is all you need to get started with Cricut accessories. A piece of standard aluminum foil for the household firmly balled up.

An aluminum foil ball will help maintain the sharp-point blades smooth and tidy and will hopefully ensure that you don't have to purchase new blades for a long, elongated time. There will be any in your nearest grocery shop, or you can order aluminum foil from Amazon.

5. Adapter for Bluetooth

The older machines from Cricut Explore did not come with Bluetooth activated. You should, however, buy a wireless Bluetooth adapter to connect in and wirelessly use your phone.

6. Kits of Tools

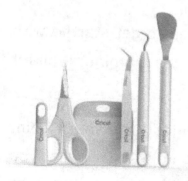

Purchasing one of the toolkits is the most affordable way to obtain the tools you would need most frequently. With tweezers, weeders, scissors, spatula, and scraper, the simple toolset comes along. This is perfect if you're mainly going to do designs of Vinyl or iron-on. All in the standard toolkit plus scoring stylus, paper trimmer, and new blade for the trimmer come with the necessary tool kit. For paper crafters, this is the dream kit.

7. The spatula

The tool you definitely should have is the spatula. You don't want to think about ripping the cloth while you're moving material off the cutting mat. The spatula takes control of this by the quick and simple removal of material from the mat. To maintain the mat clean and clutter-free, the spatula could also be used with the scraper.

8. The Tweezers

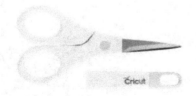

They are super handy if you don't have tweezers, though. The tweezers for weeding are the Needle Point Tweezers from Pazzles. Such tweezers have a sharp edge, which makes Vinyl outstanding. Without trying to use the edges, certain points are intense enough to grab Vinyl right from the center. Even they will pick up the smallest tiny scrap!

The other tweezes are specifically built to pick up and keep objects in place. The Cricut Tweezers are no more marketed individually but are sold in the Essential Tool Package only. If you're still looking for a decent pair, the Craft Tweezers EK tools are efficient! They are perfect for using reverse activity to pick up rhinestones as well as other adornments. It's a perfect reversal action because you don't get sore palms.

9. Scissors

A world of improvement can be created with the proper scissors for the task. The Cricut Scissors are crafted with blades of polished stainless steel, making even cuts while staying robust.

The scissors are very sharp and equipped with a mico-tip blade, so it's quicker and easier to focus on the intricate points in smaller areas right down to the point. It also has an adjustable, secure, colored end cap, which makes it easier to comfortably store the scissors. In a variety pack that contains 8" fabric scissors and 5" art scissors, Cricut offers the scissors.

The Cutter Bee Accurate Scissors are an awesome replacement to the Cricut brand scissors. For years, they've been my mom's and my go-to craft scissors, and they're still really sharp.

You'll want to get a specific pair of fabric scissors if you intend to undertake several fabric projects. With drab scissors, nothing is harder than having to cut cloth, but nothing amplifies scissors quicker than paper.

10. Cutters/Trimmers for Paper

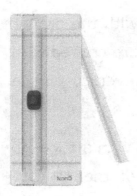

When you try to get direct cuts, a paper cutter is only super convenient. Do not use a ruler and scissors anymore. A paper trimmer, particularly while you

Are dealing with Vinyl, makes cutting so much simpler. Cricut has a trimmer of its own, but the Fiskars Sure Cut Paper Trimmer is a little more advanced. To get the ideal folds, it also has the choice of scoring.

11. Brayer

You'll want to buy yourself a brayer whether you're dealing with a cloth or bigger Vinyl (or something, really). One of the most popular mistakes that beginners make is not thoroughly stabilizing material before cutting, to learn what other top mistakes are in my post. By letting the material adhere to the Cricut mat despite harming it, a brayer solves this.

Using firm, even pressure, you run straight the roller over the material on the cutting mat to get it to hold properly and eliminate any wrinkles. It may also be used in a number of other applications, such as vinyl or ink-blocking applications.

12. Additional Mats

Something that you can have a backup or are mats as well. When you are in the midst of the task and know the mats are no stickier, there's nothing more irritating. There are places to stick the cutting mats that could save money but keeping extra mats on hand is always a smart idea.

For the kinds of mats, you use more often, you'll want extra mats. Make sure that you get mats with the correct material:

LightGrip (Blue) - for projects on paper and cardstock

StandardGrip (Green) - for iron and Vinyl

StorngGrip (Purple) - For poster board, dense cardstock as well as other heavier fabrics,

FabricGrip (Pink) - For fabric

BrightPad

For a number of factors, the BrightPad is superb. First, by having the cut lines clear, it allows weeding so much simpler. If you have more than a quick cut, lots of that can work out. For tracking and modifying designs, you may also use it.

4.2 Cricut Supplies

CARDSTOCK

You'll need cardstock while the need to start doing paper craft items with the Cricut precise towards the way. Paper-filled 12x12 scrapbook paper storage organizer

VINYL

You'll need Vinyl whether you want to begin and producing vinyl projects instantly with the Cricut. For a

number of vinyl designs. If you want to produce posters, car window stickers, coffee mugs and bottles, these are the things you'll want.

Permanent Vinyl-great even over wears and tear for designs you want to continue.

Adjustable Vinyl-good for projects that you don't want to last forever. Excellent for rentals and much more!

Glitter Vinyl-Removable Sparkle Vinyl

Dry Erase Vinyl-ideal for tagging

Chalkboard Vinyl-great for calendar creation or even for marking

If you choose to make handmade signs or screen printed shirts, use this Stencil Vinyl.

Holographic Vinyl-same as standard Vinyl, except with varying colors based on the position you are looking at

Printable vinyl-great for sticker creation

Patterned Vinyl apply some interesting themes to your projects, from Mickey & Minnie to Star Wars, watercolor and adorable hippos.

Such Material Packs are perfect if you're trying to get a selection of pieces! They come with a range of tools for cutting, tools and some even come with a Cricut cutie.

ADHESIVE FOIL has a pleasing shine to it, comparable to Vinyl. It can be tougher to weed/apply. If you're new to dealing with Vinyl, before you start using foil, use plain Vinyl.

IRON-ON-This is what you're going to use for shirts, cushions, caps, etc.

Everyday Iron-On, perfect for about every project to use! The most compact and accessible in several colors and packs

Bring sparkle to every project with **Glitter Iron-On**. Very quick to weed and to add

Holographic Iron-On: Add dimension either with opal holographic or holographic glitter to your designs

Foil Iron-On-To your designs, add shine.

Patterned Iron-On, apply those interesting designs to your projects, from Mickey and Minnie to Star Wars, watercolor and adorable hippos.

Stretchy iron-on, perfect to use on athletic apparel, Sport Flex Iron-On

Making every shirt look like a sweater, **Mesh Iron-On**,

Iron-On Prototypes-pre-made designs that can be used alone or tailored to some kind of iron-on style.

INFUSIBLE INK

NEWEST product from Cricut. To infuse ink onto clothes, tote bags and more, Infusible Ink involves heating from an Easy Press and Heat Press to send you a professionally designed project with results forever! Read more online on how it operates.

- Infusible Sheets for Ink Transfer

- Infusible Pens and Markers with Ink

- Blanks of Infusible Ink

Good for creating invitations, gift bags, gift boxes, and scrapbooking.

CARDSTOCK

Good for creating jewelry, key chains, hair bows, and infant moccasins.

FAUX LEATHER.

GENUINE LEATHER-great for creating a home furniture, shoes, and more.

FELT is best for designing finger marionettes, adornments, masks and bandanas.

WINDOW CLING is great for walls, refrigerators and other equipment for temporary tasks.

FABRIC-FOR CRICUT MAKER ONLY-fabric bundles that are suitable for every sewing project.

14. THE TAPE USED FOR TRNSFEREING-TRANSFER TAPE

The Vinyl design projects will require a minimum of one transfer tape roll to enable you to transfer the Vinyl to the surface of the project. Be guaranteed to get the Standard Grip Tape for Cricut, not the transfer tape of Strong Grip (that is just used for shimmery Vinyl).

15. EXTRA CRICUT MATS

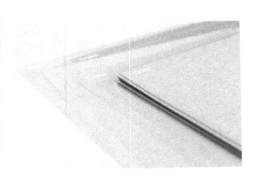

In order to function properly, certain designs may really require a fresh or relatively new mat, which is quite soggy. You should wash them; it is preferred that you partake a minimum of one of the mats used by Cricut, and if you want to undertake some bigger projects, maybe any of the 12" x 24" mats. Cricut has a range of mat packs that include 12 "x12" Light, Basic and Firm Grip mats. In 12" x24" or in multi-packs, you can even get them extra-long. Just be sure you have the correct mat for the device and supplies. In contrast to Explore and Maker, the Cricut Joy uses unique mats.

16. CRICUT EASY PRESS

The Easy Press is a perfect accessory if you're trying to do iron-on vinyl designs, which makes things easier.

17. PENS USED FOR CRICUT

Pick up a couple of Cricut pens while you ponder, you're going to try to do some envelope wrapping or inscription in common. The apt accurate in the accessory clasp. They even work on tags and designs of cards for writing.

What you need to get started with Cricut accessories are Cricut pens!

Cloth and fabric labeling pen

You'll notice it cuts fabric very well if there's a Cricut Maker. So, a limited stock of felt as well as other fabrics might be handy! You would also dearth to buy the pen for fabric marking.

And if you might be tempted, you don't need any color and form of cardstock and Vinyl.

18. Cricut Access

A trial version of Cricut Access is a catalog of photos, ventures, and fonts that comes with your latest Cricut cutting machine. It's all within the software Cricut Design Studio (the software you used or are going to use to configure your Cricut). Thus, it's advised that you select Ventures, pick 'Cricut Access subscription' from the top drop-down menu and choose a task that guises like what you want. Certain ventures will be tougher to do.

Every card is a double-sheeted project, but you'll have to freight additional mat into the machine with some other piece of cardstock. Design Space can display to you which color is going to be cut subsequent, or you may choose any colors you choose.

You may find several free SVG archives, or you might purchase them, too. Many of the archives (SVG) in the resource library are free to copy and to be used.

Chapter 5: DIY Cricut Projects

5.1 How to Start Your First Project?

Cricut offers a whole new universe of compossibilities, whether you're trying to take the paper crafts to the next juncture or make personalized clothes and décor. Cut, compose and score your creative creations with the Cricut Explore and Maker machines on a massive variety of materials: cardstock, fabric, iron-on vinyl, wood, plastic, tracing paper & more.

We are natural artists with imaginations who can create incredible and extraordinary possessions. The device can support the development of these excellent crafts. A Cricut is a smooth cutting machine used in the manufacturing of crafts. Simple Paper, Washi Sheets, card stock, vinyl, faux leather, plastic & more would be cut. Yeah, the stuff you can do with a machine from Cricut.

What do you intend for the Cricut machine to start operating?

Design Space Program is used by Cricut machines and is very simple to understand. To run the program, youwould require an Android or Apple- device, tablet, or smartphone.

5.2 Which Is The Right Cricut For Beginners?

The Cricut machine (Explore Air 2) is the perfect cutting machine for novices, advanced and skilled crafters, according to user reports. It proposes covenant software learning, fresh cutting, and excellent group support and suggestions focused on projects.

For the novice, Cricut enables crafting quite enough easier. Think about each minute that you save from doing the whole cutting and drafting for you handled by a machine. Beginner Cricut crafts and intermediate Cricut crafts are approved, yet all crafts and inventions created with the Cricut machine are sure to be magnificent. It might seem complicated the 1st time you attempt anything, but these simple Cricut ventures for newcomers are fantastic.

It's nice to be willing to give someone a handmade present. This is rendered super simple by the Cricut machine, and the choices as a novice are endless. Following are a couple of perfect novices Cricut ventures great for presents.

1. FLOWER CORSAGE

You will need the mentioned supplies to make a flower

Things you need

- Cardstock (in your color choice for flowers and leaves) (in your color choice for flowers and leaves)

- The Glue

- SCISSORS

- Pins or ribbons

- Template for Free

Directions

1. Print the template on your card stock color choice and cut the flower template. To quickly cut these, we use Cricut Explore.

2. Spray the paper gently with water (this will make it much easier to fold the paper into the forms you want) and curve the paper to form shapes.

3. On each flower segment and leaves, glue the tabs together and allow them to dry.

4. Using watercolors or markers, apply bright edges (optional). Weld together all the petals and leaves to create a flower and let it dry.

5. If you make a wrist corsage, cut the appropriate length of the ribbon, bind to the ribbon with the finished flower

6. Put one on the rear of the flower for gift-giving if you are using pins. Cover a cellophane bag or a keepsake box with the completed corsage.

This flower corsage is a simple, economical way to offer your mom a lovely, handmade present. Surprise her and make her day with this imaginative present.

2. DOLLAR STORE BURLAP FALL WREATHS

Things you need

- Straw Wreath, Noodle Pool or Wreath Foam

- Ribbon Burlap

- Free Printable or Your own or Cricut Embellishments

- Sewing Pins of Glass Head

Directions

1. Grab materials.

2. Wrap the burlap cloth across the straw wreath.

3. For the straw wreath, tie the edges of the ribbon.

4. Cut the available pintables by hand and use a Cricut and make a link

5. To tie flowers or bats and the moon to the wreath, utilize push pins.

6. Add ribbons and hang them anywhere in your house.

3. DIY COFFEE MUG

Things you need

- Cricut Explore/Machine for silhouette cutting

- 12 x 12 Cutting Mat for Cricut

- SVG file

- The Permanent Vinyl

- Tape for transferring

- Mugs for Coffee

Directions

1. Gather supplies for more details

2. Use your Cricut or Model cutting machine to cut the SVG picture (or your own image), then weed the picture.

3. Attach the transfer tape to the weeded picture, peel the vinyl paperback, and pull firmly on the mug with the image.

4. Peel the transfer tape back, and you're done!

Now you learned how to create a personalized mug with Cricut and how to use a Cricut machine to make a coffee mug.

4. DIY PIECE OF MY HEART PUZZLE CARD

Things you need

- Explore Cricut Machine Cutting

- The software of Cricut Design Space

- Jen Goode-designed Puzzle & Card

- Standard Grip Cricut® mat 12'' x 12''

- Cardstock in White and Red

- Glue

Directions

1. Print and cut the heart pattern, following the directions on the screen.

2. Assemble the puzzle and draw on the back of your own private message. By using the soft stick mat, you will briefly keep the puzzle together (the blue one).

3. Organize the envelope and inside put the components of the puzzle.

5. DIY MINI CHRISTMAS BOX AND BOW

- Cricut Machine & Cricut Design Space

- Cardstock in different colors

- ADHESIVE

Directions

1. Upload the SVG cut file gift box to Cricut Design Space.

2. Measure to the dimensions of preference.

3. Fold and glue to the end of the main body flap, and then fold it into the tabs.

4. Fill it with something you'd like.

5. Tabs to Fold Top. If you'd like, glue them together.

6. Attach a bow and ribbon.

7. Glue together the edges of each bow loop to attach the bow. To make each layer of loops for the bow,

261

glue the centers respectively. Add a second layer of loops for it. Glue the bow's back, and then wrap it in position with the tiny centerpiece and glue.

6. DIY HELLO SUMMER KITCHEN TOWEL

Things you need

- Machine for cutting Cricut Maker

- Account for Cricut Design Space

- Jen Goode's Triple Scoop Cake Cone Cut Template

- Fine Tip Blade

- Easy Press 2

- Access to Cricut Design Space

- Three shades for the scoops & one for the cone, Iron on Kitchen Towel for Kitchens

Directions

1. Open the Space Cut File for Arrangement and scale it to match the kitchen towel.

2. Ungroup the pic.

3. Highlight each part and pick the file to cut. The drawing portion of this cut file has to be deleted.

4. Add the text above the ice cream cone and below it.

5. Curve the text above the cone using the curve function.

6. Give a cut to the project. On a standard grip cutting mat, put the iron on it. Until you cut, don't forget to mirror the pic.

7. Weed the surplus iron-on and repeat with each color.

8. Pre-Heat Easy Press 2 as per the heat settings suggested by Cricut.

9. On the towel, put the ice cream cone and press it in place. Layer the scoops of ice cream on top of the cone one at a time. Then, just include the text.

7. DIY MAGNETIC CHORE CHART

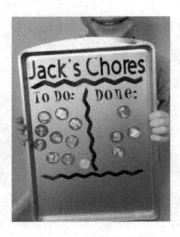

Things you need

- Cookie sheet

- Flat-edge translucent glass marbles, 1''

- You will need some sort of transparent adhesive if you are using marbles.

- Epoxy Magnet Paper (just make sure that it would be small enough for your machine to cut.

- Printable Paper for Sticker

- Blade with the Deep Cut

- Adhesive Vinyl or Adhesive Foil of the chosen color

- Transferring Tape

- A project of Design Space for Magnets and Vinyl

Directions

1. Open and configure the Design Space Project. You should modify the name, font used, etc., in this file until we get underway (or add different chores).

2. Follow these guidelines on how to use Cricut to create magnets. You can miss the section about making them and go to step four right away.

3. You will then cut out the remainder of the project with vinyl or sticky foil using your fine point blade until you cut out the magnets.

4. Once the components are cut out, the residual material is weeded out.

5. And transfer the stuff to your cookie tray using transfer tape.

6. And now, you're done.

5.3 Tips and Tricks for Cricut Projects

It can be super daunting to start off as a novice user of Cricut. You have no idea what to do, what you need to know, and where to get started. These Cricut tips are some excellent hacks from professional crafters that would save you significant money and stress as you don't have an infinite budget or time. Check out the ones

1. Prior to your first use, prepare the Standard Grip mats.

In reality, if you placed paper right on that mat, you can end up ripping the paper when you attempt to eliminate it. These green mats can be quite sticky. Your mat seasoning could make a huge difference.

Why are you seasoning a cutting mat for Cricut? Simply put on the mat a sheet of plain paper, clean it down, and carry it up. Repeat a couple of times to make sure you are making your way around the whole mat. This will help minimize the mat's initial "bite," which can be very harsh and destroy your materials, particularly the paper projects!

2. To make it wear uniformly, move your mat.

With the silhouette arrow (also the dangling position) pointing toward the machine, most Cricut users load the mats. But, with time, the plastic can wear down and allow it to crack, and it has to be changed.

- **How to make it last longer with the Cricut mat?**

Rotate it in order to prolong the life of the mat. Try to alternate aiming the tiny silhouette arrow often to the machine AND other times to yourself. Anyway, the mat may load, and this will actually increase the Cricut mat lifetime. Just try to ensure that the supplies are still mounted in the upper left corner on whichever hand you have pointed to your machine.

3. How to use a broken or damaged Cricut mat?

Does it have a break in your mat, so you just need to have one more cut out of it? With these mats, cracks, cuts, and normal wear and tear or just realities of life, this is, after all, a cutting machine. And what if the mat isn't yet ready for you to get out of? Or what if you only need yet another cut out of it.

Mark a piece of tape on the rear of the mat. Trying to cover the damaged section entirely. This, at least briefly, will help stabilize it, so you can begin the idea.

4. How to install a bounding box to promote weeding projects?

Attach a bounding box to the IN Design Space Studio. Whatever fits better for your design, cover your design with a box or circle in the Canvas process.

This would carve an outline around the design such that the negative stuff is simpler to weed away from the design.

5. Do you have a lot of little, complicated information to weed out of your project?

A substitute for the weeding of minor information from the project. To collect all those little bits, try running a gunk roller over the project.

Might not get most of them, and it might get more than you expect, particularly on very complicated projects, sparing you a bunch of time and energy.

6. Stop stressing and worrying, if the setting you have selected is right, if the stress is appropriate, etc.

Only turn it over to Custom. It's a set-and-forget plan that works beautifully.

This helps you to directly pick the settings in Design Space and adjust them from there.

7. Want to dip the toes into the making of stencils without losing precious resources such as vinyl or acetate?

With your Cricut, you may cut stencils out of freezer paper. This is a perfect, inexpensive stencil choice and is something that you probably have in the kitchen already.

Best of all, you have many more if anything goes bad, because compared to other materials such as vinyl and acetate, it costs pennies.

8. Using Glad Press 'n Seal as a really cheap replacement rather than transferring paper

This is a terrific hack in a mess. Using contact paper, which works well for moving photos for around $5 on Amazon and at Walmart, is a perfect budget-friendly alternative that works even more.

9. Remove small pieces with a gooey lint roller from the Cricut cutouts.

A lint roller may also be used to clear glitter from the cutting mat and tends to hold them sticky at the very same time! Sincerely, this is like a hack from 3-for-1.

10. Cheap way for the Cricut Mat to clean up

The best method of washing mats efficiently and conveniently is just basic Daily cleaner and hot water. Or, choose a non-alcoholic baby wipe if it's only a short cleanup. Some persons, however, stand by Awesome spray (yep, that's the brand name) that you can purchase at the Dollar Store.

11. How to get the mat sticky again?

It will look SUPER sticky when you first use your mat. It will start losing the stickiness over time, however, but this is a perfect trick to make it last longer so that you don't have to fix them so much (saving money again!)

Simply tape your mat using painter's tape off the sides and gently spray this fantastic stuff on your mat to bring the sticky back.

Recent mats are really too sticky. Before the first task, you might also want to rub your hands all across them several times to help "wear" them in. Always make sure that the correct mat is used. Initially, the green mat would be too messy for the cardstock, so you'll want to choose the blue mat.

12. Using a credit card / older gift card to rub the layout well for an easy transfer following weeding if you lose your burnishing method.

13. To produce a stencil that is basically free, cut freezer paper with your Cricut. A nice trick if, for instance, you want to create a wooden sign.

14. To avoid pet hairs or dust from clinging to them, hold the plastic sheet that corresponds with your mats and place it back on after usage.

15. To quickly extract scraps while weeding, wrap covering up or painting tape across your palm.

16. Label the top of your mat to prevent errors:

To make sure you load it right, label the upper part of your cutting mat. This is essential for beginners to prevent costly faults that could involve cutting thru your mat if improperly loaded!

17. with the latest fonts, spice up the layouts.

At dafont.com, find a Lot of free options. If you use them on items you sell, you may require a certificate for professional use. Just be cautious.

5.4 How to Sell Your Cricut Products

Few Tips for making money With Cricut.

1. Intended to be unique

In general, just be yourself. Bring to the table your strangeness and innovation. In the designing universe, that's how it works, isn't it? But you may be one of the first individuals to get on a wave trend ride before the next popular seller comes along. But if you're not patient, the process of selling Cricut crafts may get tiresome and expensive.

Upgrade your crafts at Cricut and put your own emphasis on increasing profit margin trends. Don't be frightened of changing fonts even. Super promotions and freebies for quality fonts can be found at fontbundles.net, something that easy would help you look professional with fonts.

And when the craft appears like someone else's, the fact is, it's only going to become a trade battle. Nobody's expecting to win.

2. Keeping it refined

You will think that producing and selling something under the sun would give you more diversity, thus more clients, hence more income. That's not the way it goes, however.

More prices, more exhaustion, and more non-selling goods are what it would bring you.

Do not aspire to be the design world's Walmart; aim to be a professional, and the best of your field of craftiness is there. So, take a moment to determine what you are going to be remembered for.

3. be impervious

Work regularly on the Cricut craft venture. Preferably, each day you can be focusing on it. Any of you might only choose to offer it as a passion and might only be willing to work once a week on it.

Do so as frequently as you can, whatever the routine is. If you neglect your businesses for days or months, or years, you're never able to get far.

Be compliant with prices and also with consistency. Your clients need to know what to demand from you. If they feel they can rely on you, they can suggest you to everyone else over and over.

4. Tenacious wins

There are bound to be days where clients piss you off. There'll be days where nothing works smoothly. You're going to bust your butt and easily going nowhere. Be courageous when you make your Cricut money; never relinquish.

5. How much do you want?

Please go through all of your materials and measure up the costs for the love of all things crafty. You'll be well able to price the goods for sale until you have the expense of materials. If you enjoy working for free, don't overlook the time it would take you to create the products.

A basic rule of thumb is that the purchase price would be between two and four times your supply cost. Don't fear because people are snickering at you that it's too much. You're the original, you've narrowed the scope down, and you're a professional, and you're the best at what you're doing. Plus, you use premium merchandise (more on that soon). People would pay for it happily.

6. Learn something new every day

Do not be ashamed of knowing about others before you have left. You don't have to find out all by yourself.

Everyone else has already accomplished it if you want to understand how to ascend the Etsy rankings or build a good Facebook community, and now they teach all the tips and techniques they know.

At least you'll be doing more advertising than crafting at the start of the Cricut Company. Making it a priority to discover something fresh that applies to your business every day.

7. Control of quality

Selling standard products. Any day of the week, quality dominates over quantities.

People are going to pay for quality, and for quality, they will suggest you to their mates. The most that you can do is the word of mouth marketing.

Conclusion

The Cricut machine is a very successful creation. It has enabled scrapbookers and many others with their desires, not only limited to the field of scrapbook making, but also to other aspects. There are several advantages of owning one of these machines, and Cricut has taken everyone by storm. The Explore and the Maker are so extremely versatile that one of these machines actually derives from a number of ventures people use with blogs or social networking.

As many people would realize and are conscious of, while crafters do a number of work that never see the light of day, they do just as many as they do, and you can still go back to certain projects later and expand them before finishing them with the saving option that this machine gives you. If a holiday has arrived and you do not have a present, or if there are last-minute activities coming up and you will need cool ideas to carry them with you, this may be a perfect choice for you.

Style is still a key concern in the scrapbook. Choosing a template in the past could cause migraines of monumental dimensions, but that is a different matter now. The Cricut machine itself is only liable for cutting papers on the basis of a particular pattern or design, Vinyl, and fabric. You may create or modify the pattern or layout via a software program called the Cricut Design Space. Go for Cricut cartridges if you are searching for simple and well-defined designs that have already been built-in. For the templates that are already in effect, there is no limit on what you may make. The basic rule is to let your creativity run wild. This is a product that any potential scrap-booker wants to have. Besides being a cutter with designs for a scrapbook, the Cricut machine has many applications.

Cricut Maker Machine

A Step-by-Step Guide to Master the cricut machine with creative project ideas

By Melissa Johnson

Introduction

The chapters in this book will cover everything from finding the Cricut machine that's perfect for you and your needs to designing stunning projects with a professional, polished appearance. Cricut will help you make designs that look so professional that consumers would want to know where their goods can be bought.

Cricut is a clever cutting instrument that can be used to build or customize almost everything you can think of. In order to get you started, we will give you everything you need to know, as well as the insider data of the most accomplished crafters using this groundbreaking tool.

There are plenty of books on the market on this topic; thanks again for picking this one! Enjoy. Every attempt has been taken to ensure that it is full of as much valuable knowledge as possible.

Chapter 1: Getting Acquainted with Cricut

In this chapter, we will discuss the basic information about Cricut Machine; it's different Models, Tools, and designs

1.1. What is Cricut?

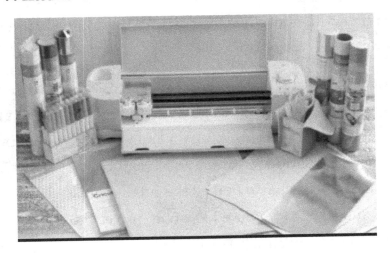

A die cutter, craft plotter, or a smart cutting machine is the common title for the Cricut. This machine's format allows you to create projects from flat materials of various thicknesses. Based on your ability level with these materials, the tasks that you can do with this product can vary from easy to very complicated. Your materials can range anywhere from craft felt to thin sheets of metal, depending on the sharpness of the blade in your cutting machine or the type you are using. This gives you an example of how wide the variety actually is, as a crafter, with what this machine will help you achieve.

You can run several hundred or even thousands of dollars on other machines of this kind, require design degrees, come with complicated proprietary software, and provide just a fraction of the design options that come with Cricut and the user-friendly, proprietary Cricut Design Space. In campaigns, tips, tricks, manuals, and new materials to use on your Cricut machine, Cricut's huge base of users are still sharing the latest and greatest. As a crafter with a machine from Cricut, the abilities are almost infinite.

I've wanted to compile the best of what's possible thanks to the huge amount of tools at our disposal as crafters, so you don't have to sift through something overwhelming before beginning to create your beautiful creations and enjoy your new Cricut machine. You'll be able to find all the details you need for how to use the app in one structured location, project guides that take you from start to finish, a list of all you'll need, and so much more. This is your thorough guide to which you can return again and again, regardless of how your level of ability improves with time!

I plan to offer you all the most useful details on the topic of Cricut, what it can do, how to get the most out of your machine, and how to get the best results consistently. In the later chapters of this book, the trade secrets illustrated would have you crafting like a specialist in no time at all. Feel free to add all your frequently asked questions, troubleshooting tips, and Cricut Hacks in chapter six of this book, so answers are still right at your fingertips.

Much as in many other media, if you're not paying attention, you might spend money on supplies, equipment, gadgets, and more than you expected. My aim is to show you the patented instruments are worth the extra cost while showing you the best alternatives you can use instead of other instruments. Crafting is such a relaxing and fun experience; thanks to the price, it should not be prohibitive! When you get acquainted with the Cricut user community, with the Cricut brand, I am sure that you can find the tools and tricks that work best for you to bring your crafts to life.

Let's delve into how to pick the best model for you and your needs for Cricut!

1.2. How to Choose the Right Model?

The best thing about Cricut is that all of their templates are unbelievably scalable and capable. The majority of features that one model has will cover the entire existing Cricut product range. The methods in which they act and the complexity of their service have certain very small variations.

I have listed all the models that are currently available from Cricut in the section below, what they do, how they vary, and which areas among certain models are better.

What's Available?

Fortunately, at the time of writing, there are not a huge amount of art plotters available from Cricut, which means it would be pretty simple for you to take a peek at all that is offered without getting frustrated. Finding what you want and need can be a real challenge, with large product lines including several different versions, while having the best with your dollar. I'm going to outline what of the currently available versions, what they can do, and what talents are better suited for what kinds of crafts.

1.3. Cricut Explore One

This is the most simple machine they sell, in terms of what is actually available from Cricut. As well as being completely user-friendly, this machine is able to cut 100 of the most common materials currently available for use in your Cricut machine.

The Cricut Explore One is known to be the Cricut craft plotter's no-frills starting platform and runs at a slower speed than the other available versions. The Cricut Explore One has only one accessory clamp inside, unlike the others present in the current model range, so cutting or scoring and drawing cannot be achieved at the same time. They should, however, be finished, one right after the other, in quick succession.

Although this is a wonderful instrument for a wide variety of crafts on 100 different materials and will get you well on your way to creating breathtaking crafts that are still a step above others, the cost is not as big as you would expect. If you intend to use your art plotter exclusively for those special occasions when it is ideal for anything handmade, then this is a fantastic machine to have on hand.

1.4. Cricut Explore Air

The Cricut Explore Air model is fitted with Bluetooth capability, has a built-in storage cup to hold your tools in one position when you are working, so they will not roll away or get lost in the shuffle, with all the features of the Cricut Explore One and more.

This model has two onboard accessory clamps, which allow for marking and cutting or scoring simultaneously. These clamps are labeled with an A and a B, so any time you load them up, you can be sure your tools are going in the right positions.

This model is designed to handle the same 100 materials as the Cricut Explore One and runs at the same pace, so those variations and similarities represent the price gap! For the powerhouse you're having, this is a big value.

1.5. Cricut Explore Air 2

The Cricut Explore Air 2 is the new top-selling craft plotter for Cricut and is arguably the greatest value for the price they have to deliver. This model cuts fabric has Bluetooth capability and has two onboard accessory clamps at double the speed of the previous two versions.

The storage cup on the top of the unit has a secondary, shallower cut to hold your replacement blade housings while they are not in service so that they are all readily accessible to you during the project if you happen to be going between multiple different tips for a project. Both cups have a soft silicone rim, so you won't have to think about the blades being rusty or scratched on your machine!

This is the right machine for the job for someone who sees himself using his Cricut with some regularity. You will be able to do your craft twice as easily, and every time, even at that pace, you will get a satisfying outcome!

The Cricut Explore Air 2 is priced almost the same as the Cricut Explore One, at $249.99 at the time of publishing. Now is the time to find the best price if you're trying to move on this.

1.6. Cricut Maker

The Cricut Maker is considered to be the flagship model for Cricut. This is the one that can do just about anything on just about any content under the sun that you can fit into your machine's mat guides. The price point is the one downside of this powerhouse model. This makes this model more prohibitive unless you want to manufacture crafts with this model that you can market. If this is your goal, you can be assured that whatever you do with this unit, every single time, will be the best of the best.

This kid will pay for himself in little to no time at all if you're selling your crafts.

This machine may be overkill for the price for the avid crafter who wants to turn up to the party with the most beautiful creations that are leaps and bounds ahead of their peers. If you're keeping up with the Joneses, of course, this is the model to use.

Really, this model has it all, and we will prove it. There is no other Cricut system with the pace the Cricut Builder has. The cuts that can be made with the exclusive precision blades that only match this system are crisper than anything from a straight knife or any artisan cutter that you might ever wish for. The blade housings simply allow you to remove the tip from the housing, mount the next one, clip it back into place, and begin to roll around your projects. In addition to this, the machine will detect the content loaded into it, so at the beginning of one of the tasks, you would not need to set the category of materials. A widespread occurrence of the other model is that the job is halfway completed before the crafter discovers that the dial is positioned incorrectly.

The unit is completely Bluetooth compatible; like any of the others, it runs with ten times as much strength as some of the other ones, has a special rotary cutter attachment that helps it to glide easily through fabrics and accuracy, and so much more.

1.6. Are There Older Models?

Yes, in a phrase. There are some older versions to make room for the Explore and Maker machines that have been phased out. For the tasks that crafters would like to do, the older machines were found to need a lot more hacks, workarounds, troubleshooting, and comprehension to get detailed or even rounded cuts.

Here is a list of some of the models you may have seen in your travels:

- Personal Cricut Electronic Cutter Machine
- Cricut Create
- Expression 1
- Expression 2
- Imagine
- Cricut Mini
- Cricut Explore

Any of these models was compliant with the Gypsy, a Cricut brand, which was not unlike the Cricut Production Room we have today. In innovating the art cutting methods, both of these machines had their triumphs.

The difficulty inherent in dealing with their machinery was the key factor that Cricut worked at overhauling when designing their newest line of models. Craftsmen's communities came together with hacks and math representatives to configure their machinery to perform exactly as they needed it to.

The Cricut Design Room helps you to be an innovator with the current line of available products, as you can be with the design process, but none of the imaginative flow is absorbed by tasks that your machine can take care of.

Updating is probably worth the money if you buy one of these machines, but if it has done you well in your crafting, there's no reason to update. Cricut has always made quality goods, and through Cricut Design Space, the cartridges containing different thematic design elements are still sponsored.

The Cricut Cartridge Adapter is a USB adapter that allows your cartridges to be imported into the Cricut Design Space so that all of your components can be accessed in a single, structured space.

1.7. What are the Tools?

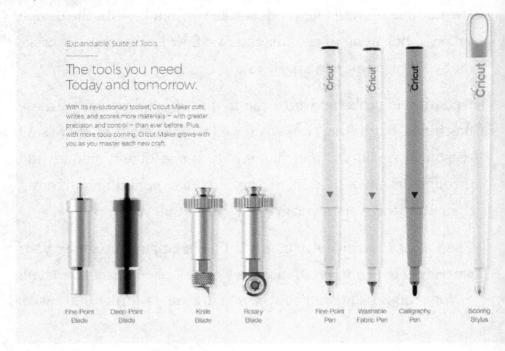

Expandable Suite of Tools

The tools you need.
Today and tomorrow.

With its revolutionary toolset, Cricut Maker cuts, writes, and scores more materials – with greater precision and control – than ever before. Plus, with more tools coming, Cricut Maker grows with you as you master each new craft.

| Fine-Point Blade | Deep-Point Blade | Knife Blade | Rotary Blade | Fine-Point Pen | Washable Fabric Pen | Calligraphy Pen | Scoring Stylus |

A brand that listens to its consumers is Cricut. Thanks to this, in order to take the project from the very outset, all the way to completion, they have thought about every single tool you might need. I've assembled a list of all the tools that help you get your projects out of and into the realities of Cricut Design Space.

Have a look at these things, get a feel for what they are, what they do, and you can see some of the ones that can be replaced by other instruments that are not part of the Cricut brand right off the bat.

You can save money by doing this, plus you will be able to use some of the materials you already have around the crafting station! Let's dive inside.

Bonded Fabric Blades

These blades are made of German carbide steel to cut with ease and consistency using bonded leather. They can be used with the FabricGripTM pad for the most effective, cleanest cuts to hold the fabric in place.

These blades, and the housings that are also available for them, are specially designed and crafted to suit the Cricut cutting machine Explore series, including the Explore Air models. The Cricut Maker wants a different blade and housing type.

1. Craft Tweezers

These reverse-action tweezers provide a good grip, fine points and relieve cramping after extended use. Throughout the project, the ergonomic grip makes it easy to maintain a firm grip on your products, giving you the extra pair of hands; you always wish you had when crafting.

2. Cricut Explore® Wireless Bluetooth® Adapter

This product lets your Cricut Explore machine connect to your monitor or tablet using Bluetooth. This useful connector makes it easier for you to apply the functionality to your Cricut Explore One machine if you have invested in the Cricut Explore One but have considered the Bluetooth features to be helpful.

3. Deep-Point Replacement Blades

Deep-point blades allow you to make deeper, more accurate cuts with ease on even thicker materials. Over time, you will find that the blades in accessory clamp B will start to become dull or simply less accurate. To resolve this, Cricut provides a line of replacement blades, and the blades will even react to sharpening before replacement on a couple of occasions.

4. Paper Crafting Set

In this package, you will find the edge distresser, quilling tool, piercing tool, and craft mat to be important in your crafts if you are especially into papercraft. These days, the art of quilling or paper filigree is more common than ever, and these are some of the best instruments available for that craft.

5. Portable Trimmer

A precision cutting tool that helps you 100 percent of the time to get fast, crisp, straight cuts on your projects is called a portable trimmer. These are extremely common with scrapbookers, so other variations of this item are largely available on the web, so keep your eye out for those with good feedback and a low price point.

6. Replacement Blades

There are replacement blades and housings on the current Cricut line that is available for any model. Any blades in the Cricut Explore line that fits the Cricut Explore One can match any model. Only that particular model would suit the blades for the Cricut Manufacturer, so be sure to read the product details or packaging to ensure you have the correct blade for you.

7. Rotary Cutting Kit

This kit comes with a gridded cutting mat and a spinning cutting tool that each time allows fast, straight, accurate cuts. Cricut is far from the only manufacturer that sells a rotary cutting product, but make sure to look at the tool and price that are better for you for other products on the market.

8. Scissors

Any crafter acknowledges that scissors are an important part of their package of tools. Although the scissors provided by Cricut are extremely sharp, with very fine points on

each blade, you would be well served here by any pair that is appropriate for your craft.

9. Scoring Stylus

The scoring stylus is intended to fit perfectly into your machine's accessory clamp A to score your projects for producing and embossing impact, folding lines, and so much more. In order to achieve the results you would like to create in your painting, the instrument can even be used freehand.

10. Scraper/Burnishing Tool

With the likely exception of the weeding tool, this basic tool would be your most-used Cricut instrument. If you lift your cut designs from the backing layer, you will find that moving them to your project surface will require even, steady pressure to beautifully burnish your projects. This tool can be replaced with other things in a hurry, but this tool does the best job, truly.

11. Spatula

When you're peeling or setting down a project, sometimes you feel like you need an extra pair of hands. This platform gives you extra assistance when you need it and maneuverability.

12. True Control™ Knife

This is a precision blade and is similar in quality and form to XACTO. This knife is very handy at any crafting station for more accurate freehand cuts.

13. Weeding Tool

This is a very fine-pointed hook that helps you to strip blanks from your cut vinyl. For most, if not all, tasks you do with your Cricut, this unit will come in handy. Without needing to stretch, fold, or struggle with your material, it allows you to remove your template from the excess material. This helps keep the design's edges crisp, tidy, and sharp at all times.

14. XL Scraper/Burnishing Tool

This offers a power level that cannot be beaten. It uniformly exerts friction and tends to remove irregular layers and air bubbles. The group of users recommends this tool very strongly.

Paper Crafts Kit- In this set, you can find the edge distresser, quilling tool, piercing tool, and craft pad to be very to your taste if you are especially into papercraft. These days, the art of quilling or paper filigree is gaining popularity, and these are some of the best resources available for that craft.

Chapter 2: Cricut Design Space

In this chapter, we will discuss Cricut Design Space for the Beginners.

2.1. How do I get started?

Cricut Design Space Program is entirely web-based technology. This means that in order to use it, you would need an active internet connection, but installing the plugin would enable you to hop in from your machine and use Cricut Design Space. You can add this plugin to any laptop or tablet, log in with your credentials, and from anywhere, as long as you have an active internet connection, you can access your designs.

The prompts will ask you what kind of Cricut system you would like to install when you first log into the Cricut Design Room. This will help the software to better connect with your machine and perfectly set out your cuts. You'll want to press the "New Project" button in the upper right-hand corner until you have done this move and your machine has found the correct unit. This is where you'll be asked to download the Cricut Interface Space Plugin installer.

For the first time, opening the Design Space Plugin Installer would prompt you to mount your machine to the Cricut unit. Establishing this link facilitates smooth contact between your machine and your Cricut system. You will be able to build projects anytime you want once this link is created. This means that you can download pictures that you have found somewhere, pictures that you have made yourself, or you can use the pictures that Cricut provides either for free or with a paid access subscription from Cricut.

The first thing you need to know about Cricut Access is that you don't need to use the Cricut Design Room for this subscription. Without ever signing up for Cricut Entry, you can make use of any part of your Cricut unit.

Depending on the premium rate you select, the advantages that one gets from a Cricut Access membership vary. At the time of writing, the Cricut Access program has three membership levels available.

Monthly - $9.99 per month

You are allowed unrestricted usage of more than 400 fonts available in the Cricut Design Space with the monthly Cricut Access membership, unlimited, unlimited use of more than 90,000 photos that you can use with any design in the Cricut Design Space, 10 percent member discounts on Cricut website sales, including products that are already on sale, as well as 10 percent license savings.

Annual - $7.99 per month (billed once annually at $95.88)

You are allowed unrestricted usage of more than 400 fonts available in the Cricut Design Space with the monthly Cricut Access membership, unlimited, unlimited use of more than 90,000 photos that you can use with any design in the Cricut Design Space, 10 percent member discounts on Cricut website sales, including products that are already on sale, as well as 10 percent license savings. All of these are available in the monthly premium service tier and have added access to the Priority Member Treatment Line, which reduces customer support wait times in half.

Premium - $9.99 per month (billed once annually at $119.88)

You are allowed unrestricted usage of more than 400 fonts available in the Cricut Design Space with the monthly Cricut Access membership, unlimited, unlimited use of more than 90,000 photos that you can use with any design in the Cricut Design Space, 10 percent member discounts on Cricut website sales, including products that are already on sale, as well as 10 percent license savings. With your yearly membership, these will be available. In addition, on all orders from Cricut's website, you get up to 50 percent discounts on approved fonts, images, and ready-to-make designs, and free-economy shipping, over $50.

If you are going to build a lot of tasks in a limited period of time, these participant incentives can be helpful. Again, in order to take advantage of the Cricut Design Room or its user-friendly user interface, it is in no way necessary for users to be Access members, but these are the major benefits you can expect if you sign up for a membership!

2.2. Your First Design

When you first open the Cricut Design Room, the first thing you'll get is a really simple tutorial on how to insert a form and how to fill a colored pattern with that shape. Go ahead and go a few times in the process so you know where the different assets and choices are, so you can insert a form into the space of the template, change the linotype, and change what the shape is packed with. Finding out how to do more projects inside the Cricut Design Room will serve as a head start for you!

There are a wealth of instructional videos for different things you can do in the design room at https://learn.cricut.com/design-space-for-beginners. Tutorials, troubleshooting, and so much else can be reviewed there.

Now that you have gotten a tentative feeling for some of the fundamentals let's run through a project and get to know the whole operation.

We're going to pick the 'Letter' option as the first move. We're going to type the word "Good Vibes" in the text box that appears and select a font you want in the Design Room. Note that there would be a cost for some of the fonts on the set. If you are browsing solely for free fonts, you should choose Device Fonts, which are the fonts that are already mounted on your machine.

Once you have selected a font that suits your vision for this project, make sure that "Linetype" is set to "cut." Once you've made sure of this, in the upper right-hand corner, you can press "Make it" and follow the prompts. If the concept looks right on the pop-up page, these next steps will be followed.

Cut a piece of vinyl that is appropriately designed to suit the style, using the dimensions at the top of the design room. Get your Cricut Maker pad in light blue or light-grip, and line up your vinyl to print your template on it. If you need to, make changes to where the concept is in the Design Room.

Using the rounded back of your scraper/burnishing tool to smooth the vinyl down on the clenched top, operating from the center out along the corners, until you get your vinyl where you need it. Make sure the piece is smooth with no bubbles or folds to ensure that you have the crispest and correct cuts possible.

On your Cricut Explore model, pick the "vinyl" setting now that your vinyl is lined up on your mat (skip this step if you have a Cricut Maker). Slide your mat under your Cricut Maker's white holding brackets. Select 'Continue' at the bottom right of the Cricut Interface Space until it is there. You'll be asked to press the double arrow button, and the site will connect with your phone. This is going to lock the mat into place.

Click it once and watch it perform its magic once the Cricut C button is blinking! Remove the mat from the machine and bring it to your carving room until the machine has done its cutting. Smooth the full surface of the vinyl on your mat using the rounded back of your scraper/burnishing tool. This will make the carrier sheet keep that you don't want to weed on the areas of your build.

Until you've rubbed the whole piece deeply, pick up the blanks around your letters using your weeding tool. The history, your O and G circles, all the stuff you don't want to stick to your laptop. Break a suitably-sized piece of transfer tape until only the letters are left on the carrier board. Smooth the transfer tape down into the entirety of the template using the back of your scraper. Peel the tape back from the carrier sheet until you've got a firm grip on the template.

Clean the area on your laptop where you want to position your template, using some rubbing alcohol. Lay the pattern where you like it until it's fully clean, and rub it into shape with the back of your scraper. To show your new template and to admire your handiwork, gently peel back your transfer cover. You've just finished your first project with Cricut.

Chapter 3: Your Cricut Materials

3.1. What Supplies Will I Need?

There are some basics that you will need in order to get started before you start working on Cricut ventures. If you're trying to do a project on adhesive vinyl, as an example, here's a rundown of what those basics are.

3.2. Your Cricut Machine

You would want to get it set up, prepared, and ready, with the fine point blade loaded into accessory clamp B, until you choose the model that is better for you from the ones mentioned in the first segment.

3.3. Cricut Machine Cutting Mat

This mat is a very basic but important part of the carving method for Cricut. There are some thin mats in Cricut, with both an adhesive grip and a grid on them. You will be confident that the content is right where it needs to be when the material is layered on this mat and placed into your Cricut system in order to achieve the ideal cuts and strokes on it.

This is one of the fabrics that is best left to the Cricut brand because of their special scale and grip strength. It might end up being more expensive, or just less successful, to search for another mat with equivalent skills.

cut settings for Cricut

Vinyl Type	Blade	Speed	Thickness
Oracal 631 Oracal 651	3	High	Medium
Glow Adhesive	3	Medium	High
Inkjet Adhesive	3	High	Medium
Glitter HTV	4	Medium	High
Foil HTV	3	Medium	Medium
Smooth HTV	3	High	Medium
Glow HTV	3	Medium	High

The Cricut brand for this unique part is really the one to go for.

3.4. Transfer Tape

Transfer tape is an adhesive tape that is smooth, gentle, and comes in tubes. The purpose of this material is to take your freshly cut designs from their backing layer, keep them securely in place tightly, which you can then quickly brush on your project. The adhesive is so that the template or the material it's supposed to go on will not be affected.

Later in this book, each time you use it, you can find some tips on how to get the best out of your transfer tape and on picking a transfer tape that you can get in acceptable grip strength, consistency, and quantity that is most ideal for your ventures.

For e.g., if you do a lot of projects on products with a very coarse or glittery surface, you would need a higher grip strength transfer tape to hold them in place when you work on them.

I'll inform you right out of the gate that the transfer tape for the Cricut brand comes in a single sheet that is folded up and measures up to 12' x 48.' In whatever size or shape that your project needs, you can cut the sheet to your taste, and each section that you cut can be used many times before disposal. For the favorite crafting store, these sheets from the Cricut brand are currently at $8.99 MSRP, while several other manufacturers sell a 6-10 "roll of 12"-wide transfer tape at a similar price.

YouTube is an invaluable site that has knowledge on the newest and greatest from the people who do these styles of crafts every day, and the best information on whose brands are best for the types of projects you want to do.

When doing projects with your Cricut machine, while transfer tape is an utter requirement, the brand is not almost as critical as getting anything to use.

As for any new art you do, identifying the materials and items that better suit your needs will wake up a little bit of trial and error and will perform best for you in the long run.

3.5. Isopropyl or Rubbing Alcohol

Since the adhesive is a key theme and part of the Cricut method and the process of operating the Cricut machine, it is important to ensure that the surfaces that you are using (the mat, the fabrics, the object on which the template would be brushed) can be washed as humanly as possible from impurities.

You would want to rub-down the surface with some rubbing alcohol, especially with a slippery surface like glass or ceramic, to remove any soil, grease, debris, or something that might damage the design. Your template will be ready to go if you clean it down with rubbing alcohol, pat it dry, and let it stand for thirty seconds!

Make careful that any paper towels or other items that you use for this phase do not leave behind any fibers or debris that could undermine your design, particularly those that are smaller or more complicated.

3.6. A Blank Stage for Your Design

This is the item onto which you'll be burnishing your design. It's important to know that while the world is your oyster and that there is very little unavailable to you with Cricut crafting, I recommend a flat surface for your first project. Being able to access the whole surface of this piece without having to worry about curvature or other obstructions will make it much easier to learn how to work with your materials.

While a travel mug is a great idea for a Cricut project, doing it as your first might give you more trouble than you may have initially anticipated. We don't want you to start yourself out with a project that will give you trouble. Instead, consider putting a personalized design or phrase on your laptop or on a binder.

3.7. A Machine with Internet Access

The Cricut Design Room can only be accessed through an active Internet connection, so it is important to ensure that your machine will have uninterrupted connectivity over the duration of the design!

You'll want to save your job occasionally, just in case the link hiccups. You would not want to gamble on any design developments in such a situation.

3.8. Self-Adhesive Vinyl

Last but not least, a piece of self-adhesive vinyl that is your favorite color and form will be needed. You will load this onto your Cricut cutting mat, and in no time at all, your template will be cut out of it!

This is all that there is to it! You're able to deal with all these things with your first self-adhesive vinyl concept!

3.9. What Materials Can I Use with My Cricut?

Cricut boasts being able to work with more than 100 products to make your creations come to life like never before, as you've probably read in this book already. The sky is the limit of what you can do with your Cricut machine, no matter which model you have selected to buy, thanks to the vast array of media that Cricut can carry to your crafting station.

Here are 100 materials that your Cricut can use without issue!

- **Printable Sticker Paper**
- **Notebook Paper**
- **Parchment Paper**
- **Photo Framing Mat**
- **Metallic Vellum**
- **Vellum**
- **Freezer Paper**
- **Metallic Cardstock**

- Flocked Paper
- Metallic Poster Board
- Corrugated Paper
- Peal Cardstock
- Glitter Paper
- Cotton Fabric
- Wool Felt
- Canvas
- Metallic Leather
- Oil Cloth
- Felt
- Faux Suede
- Flannel
- Denim
- Cardboard
- Shimmer Paper
- Pearl Paper
- Craft Paper
- Photographs
- Cardstock
- Temporary Tattoo Paper
- Copy Paper
- Washi Sheets
- Scrapbook Paper
- Post Its

- Burlap
- Duck Cloth
- Leather
- Faux Leather
- Foam
- Glitter Foam
- Craft Foam
- Foil
- Fabric
- Polyester
- Linen
- Printable Fabric
- Silk
- Aluminum Foil
- Embossable Foil
- Aluminum Sheets
- Foil Poster Board
- Foil Embossed Paper
- Adhesive Foil
- Foil Iron-On
- Foil Acetate
- Paper
- Poster Board
- Contact Paper
- Metallic Paper

- Glitter Cardstock
- Solid Core Cardstock
- Flocked Cardstock
- Paper Board
- Tissue Paper
- Rice Paper
- Construction Paper
- Washi Tape
- Paper Grocery Bags
- Adhesive Cardstock
- Wrapping Paper
- Plastic
- Shrink Plastic
- Transparency Film
- Duct Tape
- Window Cling
- Magnet Sheets
- Plastic Packaging
- Stencil Material
- Printable Magnet Sheets
- Vinyl
- Holographic Iron-On
- Removable Adhesive Vinyl
- Flocked Iron-On
- Neon Iron-On

- Matte Vinyl
- Metallic Vinyl
- Stencil Vinyl
- Outdoor Vinyl
- Adhesive Vinyl
- Printable Vinyl
- Printable Iron-On
- Glitter Vinyl
- Glossy Vinyl
- Glossy Iron-On
- Chalkboard Vinyl
- Matte Iron-On
- Glitter Iron-On
- Permanent Adhesive Vinyl
- Dry Erase Vinyl
- Holographic Vinyl
- Metallic Iron-On
- Paint Chips
- Wood
- Chipboard
- Wood Veneer
- Adhesive Wood
- Corkboard
- Balsa Wood
- Birch Wood

3.10. What Can My Cricut Do?

There's actually no limit on how much you can do with your machine at Cricut. If you're short of reflections, though, here are some I've put together to get your creative juices going!

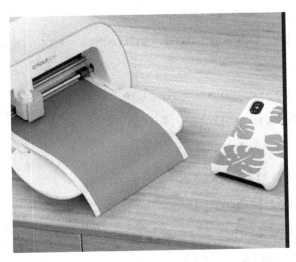

Take a browse at this page and come up with any things you think are going to suit perfectly with the kinds of designs you want to make!

- **Make felt dolls**
- **Beautifully address envelopes**
- **Create doll clothing**
- **Make greeting cards of every design and style**
- **Create placards**
- **Cut items out of balsa wood**
- **Cut washi tape shapes**
- **Craft borders and decorations for your corkboard**

- Dream up refrigerator magnets
- Customize wedding invitations
- Create holiday crafts
- Design or decorate purses and wallets
- Cut your own craft foam shapes
- Create decals and patterns for pillows and cushions
- Create your own coloring book pages
- Cut fabric with precision
- Make jewelry
- Make party favors
- Create 3D bouquets
- Cut leather
- Cut your own party hats
- Make themed window clings
- Create fabric appliques
- Create temporary tattoos
- Create glassware decals
- Design personalized gift tags
- Create clothes for your pet
- Create custom gift boxes
- Customize baby clothes
- Design creative pincushions
- Create cake toppers
- Customize holiday ornaments

- Custom Coasters
- Create sewing patterns
- Create themed t-shirt transfers
- Make personalized fabric key fobs
- Cut perfect quilting squares
- Create and embellish your own holiday stockings
- Craft decorations to fit any theme
- Design dust covers
- Cut unique stencils
- Create stickers & decals
- Design Door Hangers
- Create jigsaw puzzles
- Add pizzazz to headbands
- Create fabric accessories and embellishments
- Cut patterns to make your own socks and embellishments
- Create wedding place cards
- Make 3D papercraft shapes
- Write beautiful signs in calligraphy
- Create cupcake flags
- Craft cushion transfers
- Design 3D and flat-panel wall art of any theme
- Cut scrapbook embellishments

Chapter 4: Cricut Projects for Beginners

In this chapter, we will discuss the different Cricut Projects for Beginners.

4.1. Technique

Patience is by far the best strategy I can give you and will help you get closer to pulling off the ideal project. Take the time to unwind, take the time to get the content to do what you want it to do, and dream about imaginative ideas. For your creations made with the Cricut method, doing so would still produce a greater rate of success. "Always go with a positive attitude into your projects that says, "I can do this!" In addition, bring a questionable attitude that asks, "Why do I do this differently? With that and a lot of maturities, you're going to find that your ventures are going to run quicker and much better. Plus, when you do it this way, you will have so much more fun!

You can find more specifics in the sections below on how to improve the efficiency of the crafts you produce and ways to work that make things run more smoothly! On the issue of maximizing the life of your accessories and components, as well as ways to use them as economically as possible, we have a lot of data to cover!

You'll find that your Cricut Explore unit comes directly out of the box with some cardstock, a pen, a blade, and a mat. The very first of your beginner's ventures will get you through these tools.

You will find that your skill level with the Cricut device will improve very quickly when you get the hang of using the Cricut Concept Space program and how the Cricut machine works. For anyone who starts with their Cricut machine, these novice projects are all just the right skill level, so choose the one you want and get to work!

4.2. Cricut Hello Greeting Card

Take off the top of your green Cricut cutting pad with the waterproof plastic coating and set it aside. Make careful to keep it not wrinkled or broken anywhere, as this is the layer you can place back on top of your mats before you store them next time.

This will ensure the adhesive finish, providing more durable strength to your mats during your designs.

With the top left-hand corner of the grip on your mat, line up your cardstock, keeping the textured side of the cardstock faced upward. Smooth your cardstock with your hands to ensure that your cardstock does not form holes, wrinkles, or folds.

Place the mat under the mat guides in your Cricut machine until you've lined up your cardstock with your mat corner. When you press the Load/Unload lever, marked by the double arrow, on the top of your unit, firmly drive the mat against the rollers.

Within your machine, open Accessory Clamp A and remove the cap from your Cricut metal pen, which came with your machine. Place the cap on your pen's back and slip it snugly into place so that you don't drop it when working. Press up softly on the bottom of the accessory clamp A when you insert the pen after you've done so. Press softly but tightly into the clamp until the clamp covers the little arrow on the pen, and you hear a click. Close the clamp and take the finger out from under it.

You will notice that you're able to launch your design now that your machine is loaded and set up with the necessary accessories. Click on the menu and choose New System Configuration if you are having trouble locating a project or if Cricut Design Space does not immediately prompt you to start this design. Follow the initial steps once more before the project for you is pulled up by the server. Alternatively, with the keyword "Phone," you can use the project search feature. This can bring up the two-layered template of the greeting card we are making here.

To ensure that the template is properly matched up with the materials on your mat, press the 'Make It' button. If this screen tells you that the design is cut in a space that your cardstock does not fill, unload the mat, change the cardstock, either reload it and return to the "Make It" screen, then return to the space of the design and adjust where the design is laid out. Once this is correctly plotted out, return the mat to the machine and return to the "Make It" screen.

To ensure that your machine is adding the right amount of pressure to your cutter, adjust the dial on the outside of your Cricut Explore machine to the 'cardstock' configuration. This will provide you with the cleanest, most detailed cuts imaginable.

Click the 'Go' button until everything seems to be in place. On your Cricut machine, give it a push until the Cricut C button starts blinking. Your machine will set itself the task of drawing the template and cutting it!

Tap the flashing Load/Unload button until that's done, and remove your mat from the Cricut unit. Open accessory clamp A, attach the pad and replace the cap to ensure that when writing, the pen won't dry out. When your pen is capped, place it in front of your machine's storage compartment. Now you are really going to know where it is!

Flip it face down on your work surface to release your work from the mat, so the back of the mat is facing you. Curl your mat's corner softly back toward you before the cardstock separates from your mat's adhesive board. Keeping the cardstock flat on the work surface with your free hand, adding pressure uniformly to prevent your project from curling when you remove it from the mat.

With the blue paper that came with your machine, fold the cardstock in half evenly, then repeat this move. Place the paper inside the card until they're both folded equally so that it shines across the cut spaces in your cardstock.

Congratulations on the very first Cricut Concept Project being done! You're doing excellent work.

4.3. Happy Birthday Gift Tag

Three different colors of cardstock of your taste, a roll-on adhesive tape, and a glue pen are special supplies for this project. If you think that it will work best for you to use other forms of adhesive, feel free to use them instead.

Visit the web application for Cricut Design Space and pick the alternative for designing a new project. Click "Images" once you're there, and check for the word "tag." Pick a shape that looks like a simple gift tag: Once you've chosen this file, you should see the queue at the bottom of your screen.

Now, at the top of the page, press the "Categories" button, and pick the "Birthday" category before setting the search filter to "Phrases." Click on the "Happy Birthday to You" picture of your choosing. We have selected the one that seems to be on a wavy flag.

You should press the green "Insert Images" button in the lower corner of your screen until you have made your pick for both images. This will connect the images to the space of your design so that you can manipulate them to suit the design you want to create.

Use the arrow button at the bottom right of the image to scale the image to the appropriate proportions. Drag the tag image closer to the upper left corner of the Cricut Design Space.

The next thing you'll want to do is to rotate the tag 90 ° with the circular arrow button so that your Happy Birthday picture can match with any quick resizing on the tag. However, if you drag the sentence over to your tag, you will find that the text disappears under the picture of the tag. This is not a concern because, at the top of your screen, you can simply click "Arrange" and pick the "Move to Front" option. This will insert the phrase over the tag of the gift so that it is easily visible.

Now, let's resize the word so that it suits with no problems on the tag properly. In the bottom right corner, press the arrow and move it until the template is sized appropriately for your project.

Let's discuss the color of your pictures now. While the Cricut machine does not print or influence the color of the materials, you are using, depending on the color of the materials in its port, it does discern where to make its cuts. Set the photos in Cricut Design Space to match the color of the cardstock you have on hand in order to keep your own thoughts clear on which cardstock to put where and to keep your Cricut cutting properly.

You can see a panel on the right side of your screen that displays every layer of your template. Simply click on the picture layer you want to change; next to the line, color options pop up. You may easily pick the color from here that suits most closely the cardstock that you have selected for this section of your project.

If two layers of your design are the same color, by consolidating all of those elements of your design into the same sheet, you can make it a little simpler in the cutting process. Only drag one layer of your template to the one you want to combine it with and remove it. This will bring all of them together, holding them the same color!

Click "Save," give your project a special name that you can know, and click "Save" again until you have had all the elements of your project to look the way you want. First, to launch the cutting process, you'll press "Make It."

The mat preview screen will show you every step of the cutting technique and where the cuts will be made on your materials. Any of these components will be color-separated, so you can see what cuts will be made on your various cardstock pieces.

If you choose to make several gift tags, simply adjust the quantity of Project Copies to your desired number, then press "Apply." This will refresh your view to show you where the cuts will be made on the different cardstock colors that you have chosen.

Photos should not be changed in any manner on the preview screen, but if at this point of the process you do have adjustments to make, actually go back to the design room, make the changes there so that the layout is set out to your standards, and return to the "Make It" screen to reassess and start the cutting process.

"Click the "Continue" button until it seems like it's set out the way you need it. The next moves in your project will prompt you to take them.

You may want to ensure at this point of the process that the material dial on the outside of your Cricut Explore machine is set to "Cardstock," ensuring that all the cuts are made as correctly as possible.

On the prompt pad, take the first cardstock that is seen and lines it up on your mat. Make careful to match up the material with the grid and the grip on the mat so that it's square. When completed correctly, it would line up with the corners of the grid. Through your fingertips, smooth the material over, ensuring that no visible cracks, wrinkles, or folds form on the material.

By slipping it below the mat directions, bring the mat into the unit. Until pressing the Load/Unload button, holding the mat tightly pressed against the rollers. Tap it and watch the machine jump into motion until the Cricut C button starts flashing.

Flip it face down on your work surface to release your work from the mat, so the back of the mat is facing you. Curl your mat's corner softly back toward you before the cardstock separates from your mat's adhesive board. Keeping the cardstock flat on the work surface with your free hand, adding pressure uniformly to prevent your project from curling when you remove it from the mat.

You can find that all that's left on the mat are your design parts after you've finished this movie and some blanks in the lettering. Using the weeding tool to remove the blanks and remove the pattern parts from the mat with the spatula.

To eliminate any leftover blanks or cut cardstock on your mat, use your Scraper/Burnishing Tool.

Load the next piece of cardstock until your mat is clear, as shown by the screen in Cricut Design Room. By slipping it below the mat directions, bring the mat into the unit. Until pressing the Load/Unload button, holding the mat tightly pressed against the rollers.

Tap it and watch the machine jump into motion until the Cricut C button starts flashing.

Click Finish in the Design Space browser window after all the parts have been cut.

It would be easier to work from the bottom layer when constructing the project, going up to the top layer. Keep the project open with the Cricut Design Space so that you can reference it as you put it together.

Protect the bottom later on the next sheet using your roll-on adhesive tape or your favorite means of adhesive.

Secure the specifics of your lettering sheet with a glue pen or your favorite form of adhesive. Mount the lettering on your tag until that is done, and you're all out!

4.4. Wooden Welcome Sign with Vinyl Designs

You would need self-adhesive vinyl, transfer tape, a weeding tool, a knife that is either the True Control or another precision cutter, your scraper or burnishing tool, a trimmer or scissors, and a plaque of wood painted or polished according to your choice for this project.

Navigate to the Cricut Interface Room and open your window. Logging in, if you are not already signed in, would be the first move. This will grant all your money, designs, and elements accessible to you. Tap "New Project" until you're signed in.

On the left-hand side, select the 'Letter' option. Once the text box comes up on your phone, type WELCOME next to the text box in the dialog box. You can see a text box filled with the same text after you have typed it.

Now, it's time to choose the font that suits this project better. Choose one that's to your taste. A plain font, sans serif, is recommended for this project. Make sure to pay attention to whether the font you have picked is paying for or not.

In a new line under your WELCOME, add some extra text that you would like on your welcome plaque. For this playful, decorative initiative, your family name or, maybe, a humorous slogan is suggested. Once you've selected that, resize your welcome to the same distance. Both text lines can be only slightly shorter than the width of the plaque of your wood.

Place all of your text boxes on the same layer, selecting the one with the best weight for your project.

To leave ample space for a wide monogram, placed some distance between the text boxes. This picture is going to go in between the text lines.

Click "Images" and set your Single Layer Images filter, then check for the "monogram" keyword. Pick the one you want and then click "Insert Images."

Place your monogram between your text layers and resize it before everything gets together.

Let's curl out the WELCOME text for some extra flourish. It will help us line up our letters equally by using a blank form as a reference for this curve. Pick the shape of the "Circle," expand it into an oval with the desired curve, and position it under your WELCOME over your monogram.

Now that we've put the guidance that we're going to delete after we're done lining up our letters, it's time to divide the letters in our WELCOME so that we can position them around the curve individually.

Click the "Advanced" tab at the top of the screen when the text is chosen and then click "Ungroup to Letters." This will allow you to position each letter individually along the curve. Be sure that the rotation of the letters is modified, so the whole term is put on the curve.

Delete your placeholder oval.

Check your text and picture and make some last-minute adjustments that you might need to make so that you fully like your template.

When all is in place, in the top menu, click Pick Everything, and in the lower right-hand corner of your screen, click Connect. There will be a little paperclip icon underneath the attach option.

You will find all layers are merged into one until that's finished. Edit the color of your photograph, now single, to fit the content.

Click "Save," name your idea, and then again, click "Save."

To launch the cutting process, press 'Make It.' this will show you where the material on your mat will be on your cuts.

Set the vinyl dial on your phone. Using the upper left-hand corner of the grip on your mat to line up your vinyl, meaning that your vinyl backing is face down. Smooth your vinyl down with your hands so that your vinyl does not shape cracks, wrinkles, or folds.

Once you have that lined up on your mat, in your Cricut unit, put the mat under the guides. When you touch the Load/Unload button (indicated by the double arrow) on the top of the unit, softly shift the mat onto the rollers.

Click and watch your project come to life with the flashing Cricut C button.

To release your mat from the unit, press the Load/Unload button until the content is completely cut. To release much of the excess vinyl from the sheet, make an L shaped cut around the template using a precision cutter. Roll up the surplus for further use and conserve it.

Until weeding, burnish the pattern using your scraper tool. When you weed, this will help the elements of your template remain attached to the carrier layer!

Now, keep the weeding tool at a slight angle, hook it around the template onto the blank vinyl and softly pick up the parts you don't need. You should pick them up side by side in a bin or in the garbage. You should cut the larger sheet of vinyl around your template until you've removed all the small negative pieces of vinyl.

In the upper left-hand corner, grip the vinyl, drawback softly, and begin to pull down diagonally into the lower right-hand corner slowly. Wait for some of the design parts that cling to the blank vinyl that you're scraping. You can softly lead certain parts of your pattern back down onto the carrier sheet using the back of your wedding hook.

When all the components of the template are left on the carrier layer, it's time to remove the transfer tape! Place the transfer tape carefully over the whole plan. Do your best to stop bubbles, but no harm can be done to you by a few here and there!

To thoroughly burnish your pattern onto the transfer tape, use your scraper tool, then peel the carrier sheet away from the transfer tape. This will leave your pattern, with the adhesive side of your vinyl visible, sticking to the transfer tape.

Place the vinyl pattern softly on your plaque to ensure that it is entirely centered before allowing the glue to touch the surface of your plaque. Using your scraper to burnish the logo on the surface of your plaque until you have it lined up just where you like it.

Now, slowly remove the transfer tape diagonally downward from the upper left-hand corner into the lower right-hand corner. If you try to carry your transfer tape with some bits of your design, simply lay it back down, burnish it again, and start peeling.

Your vinyl production should be shown on the front of your wooden plaque proudly now!

Chapter 5: Beginner Cricut Project Ideas for Business

In this chapter, we will put forth several Cricut project ideas for beginners who aim to start a business using a Cricut machine.

5.1. Centerpieces

Any large-scale event might benefit from themed centerpieces!

5.2. Clothing

With Cricut and the numerous materials, they have to offer, put your creative flourish on anything you own. There's no amount of ways to please, whether it's an iron-on decal or a cloth embellishment!

5.3. Coasters

Coasters will make such a perfect present for housewarming or holidays, like so many other items on this page. A special set of coasters should be used by anyone to keep their surfaces clean and dry!

5.4. Coffee Mugs

Coffee mugs are definitely the one dish in my house that, when I see them, I will always want more of. They're nice for so many things, and you're the ideal addition to every office or kitchen with things that are original.

5.5. 3D Wood Puzzles

You may have seen these in museum gift shops or in the section of the toy store for the brainy kids. These are amazing fun, and they make such a great final product when put together.

5.6. 3D Foam Puzzles

Foam is just as sturdy for 3D puzzles, and you can take them apart, put them back together, knock them down, and more and they bounce right back. These make such a great gift for young children.

5.7. 3D Wall Art

Art that bounces off the wall and makes a message to all your friends about who you are is what individuals spend a lot of money to get. Place on your wall a little bit of your artistic self and show your imagination off!

5.8. Aprons

The apron is a perfect way to give a customized touch to your experience if you have a lot of enthusiasm in the kitchen. You can completely own the kitchen with a character you enjoy, an amusing saying, or simply a monogram.

5.9. Banners

With a flag, every occasion is made more formal! With Cricut, you can use your materials to create a special banner that will celebrate the event at hand beautifully.

5.10. Beanies

A knit cap is a perfect way to stay warm for any outdoor exercise that will occur during the winter months. Getting one emblazoned on the side with your own logo is sure to not only elevate the hat's theme but to make everyone wonder where they can get one exactly like it!

5.11. Bookmarks

Such a basic craft is bookmarks, but they are almost always required! Everyone near you is in the middle of reading a book at all times if your circle is like mine. Replace something nice and intimate with the shopping receipt in the center of their book!

5.12. Bumper Stickers

Anything to occupy the drivers in traffic behind you will still be in style. Create some nice comments to stick on the bumper for you and your mates!

5.13. Business Cards

Business cards that are cut from premium stock and in unique shapes can be so expensive. Printing your designs on cardstock with a standard printer and cutting out dynamic designs is sure to catch the eye of potential customers.

5.14. Cake Toppers

Got a themed birthday party coming up? Use plastic or metal to make a beautifully themed cake topper that will blow away your guests!

5.15. Calendars

No matter how the times progress, you always need to know what day it is! See what unique calendars you can make for your desk or office!

5.16. Labels

If an organization is your forte, using Cricut can help you make gorgeous labels for every room of the house!

5.17. Luggage Tags

Never be unsure of which bag on the carousel is you. Make a luggage tag that stands apart from the crowd as much as you do, and claim your bag in no time!

5.18. DIY Craft Kits

With the Cricut, producing crafting kit components is a breeze. Let your imagination run wild on the bits you should bundle together to make your own crafting ideas for others! As they make great party favors, presents for kids or crafters, and so much more, let your imagination run wild on this one!

5.19. Envelopes

Did you know that one continuous sheet of paper that is only sliced, folded, and glued in a particular way is made of envelopes? This means you can take whatever sheet of paper you want and make an envelope out of it with any print you want!

5.20. Flowerpots

A flowerpot can be sort of a mundane piece. However, with some craft paint and a stencil that you made with your Cricut, or with a decal, they can transform into something that fits your décor perfectly!

5.21. Framed Affirmations

This is a difficult life! Affirmations you can bring in your own font or theme can make all the difference from a personal room in the vibe you receive. Jazz up and bring your own all over your room!

5.22. Gift Card Envelopes

These can be accomplished with scrapbooking paper, building paper, foil paper, or, actually, something. This tiny little gift can be elevated into something deeply personal that everyone would love to have.

5.23. Party Invitations

Who's coming to your party? Everyone, because your invitations were gorgeous and now everyone is excited. Slam dunk.

5.24. Wedding Table Numbers

No matter the size of the style, the Cricut can help you to make any shape or style to fit your theme!

5.25. Personalized Clipboards

If you're an organization fanatic like myself, clipboards are pretty special objects, and having one that says the right things on the back just seals the deal.

5.26. Sealing Stickers

Elevate your letters and other mail with a beautiful sticker that tells everyone the letter is from you with love.

5.27. Stickers

Stickers are great for so many different things. Marking dates in your calendar or planner, gifts for kids, reminders, decorating your envelopes, decorating memos, giving feedback on schoolwork, and so much more.

5.28. Travel Mugs

All right, coffee mugs, yet to go. So, they are much better than coffee mugs that you can never get too many of, so you also go nuts with them.

Chapter 6: FAQs, Troubleshooting, and Cricut Hacks

In this chapter, we will discuss FAQs, Troubleshooting, and Cricut Hacks for Beginners.

6.1. Frequently Asked Questions

This segment discusses the most frequently asked questions about the experience of Cricut, as well as some of the most common issues that arise in the process. If you need an answer that you can't find here, the internet will be an incredibly helpful platform for answering almost all questions, troubleshooting most issues, and generally having a deeper understanding of your Cricut system.

Why can't I weed my design without it tearing?

This kind of problem has two fairly typical triggers. Number one is blades that are rusty. Later on in this segment, we have some ideas on how to sharpen your knives, so just look for that! The second cause for this is the deposition of residue on your blades. For tips on how to clean your blades as well, look deeper in this line!

Is it necessary to turn all my images into SVGs?

No, whether you have JPG or PNG, it is not important to convert your files to the SVG format. However, there are many free online tools that can assist you with this method if you wish to use SVG files in your project. Try to bear in mind that you will have less ability to modify the components of your image if you transform your file form to an SVG.

Where do I go to buy materials?

There is almost an infinite number of outlets where you can get them when it comes to ordering supplies for your Cricut. As the Cricut is such a powerful machine with the potential to cut so many fabrics, without tripping over new materials you can use for your latest and greatest creations, you would not be able to walk into any crafting or fabric shops.

You will find which products and labels better suit your needs as you begin to learn more about how Cricut runs and what you can do with it. From there, when searching online, you can always find what you need to get the cheapest prices and amounts of the items you prefer, which can help you spread the dollar as best as you can.

Do I need a printer to use my Cricut?

The answer in a word is No. It does not require ink from a printer to use the Cricut with the materials we have set out in this book, although there are certain materials on the market for Cricut that are clearly designed to be printed before use.

If you don't use these things, then without that feature, you can find that you can get the best out of your machine.

This is referred to as the Print and Cut approach if you want to print items, then cut them, and there is a wealth of information on the internet about this. You can make decals, tattoos, and so many more from iron-on!

Where can I get images to use with my Cricut?

The best thing about the Cricut Design Room and its capacity to host so many different types of files is that, as long as you have the legal rights to use the document, you can upload images from any source.

Do I have to buy all my fonts through Cricut?

When browsing at your fonts, Cricut Design Space has the option of using fonts that are mounted on your machine. This is called "System Fonts." You can buy or download Ant font with little or no problems from Cricut Design Room. On the internet as well, there are many outlets for this.

However, if you choose a font, make sure you have permission to use the font for the reasons that you have in mind for that font! Fonts have copyrights, much like photos, and can be restricted to what they want you to do with them.

Why is my blade cutting through my backing sheet?

This can be attributed to incorrect seating in the housing on the weapon, so just pop out the housing, re-seat the interior of the blade, refill and try again. This may also be attributed to the incorrect setting on the dial of the content. Your needle could plunge right through the whole piece of material and its backing if you cut anything really small, but have the dial set to cardstock!

Why aren't my images showing up right on my mat?

When you press Make It, it's likely that your project's print preview doesn't look like the way you have it planned out in the Design Room. If this is the case, go back to the Design Room, highlight all your pictures, press "Group," then click "Attach." This should hold it correct with all your project cutting needs where it needs to be!

I'm just getting started. Do I need to buy all of Cricut's accessories right away?

No, you won't need any of the accessories right at once, and depending on what crafts you want to do for your Cricut machine, some of them you won't ever need at all. In fact, when you get more use out of your machine, you can use crafting things you possibly already have on hand to get started, buying equipment and accessories here and there! It is, by no way, appropriate to spend a small fortune just to do your first Cricut crafting project on accessories and instruments!

Which Cricut machines at compatible with design space?

All the motorized cutting machines they have on the market are the Cricut ones that are actually compatible! The Cricut Explore, Cricut Explore Air, Cricut Explore Air 2, and the Cricut Maker imply this. With the latest edition of Design Room, you can use all these resources to build endless designs for every theme and every occasion. In order to see if they are compliant, old equipment would need to be checked with the application, as Cricut issues the application with frequent changes that could nullify the reliability over time.

Do I need to be connected to the internet to use design space?

A web-based framework that uses the cloud is Cricut Architecture Room. Because of this, to make use of the framework for your designs, you need an active, high-speed Internet connection. However, from every laptop, everywhere in the world, the cloud feature allows you access to your account, your projects, your components, and anything inside the Design Room, as long as you have an internet connection and your account credentials.

Is my operating system compatible with Cricut Design Space?

Currently, Cricut Interface Room is compatible with machines running on the new Windows, Linux, Android, and iOS

347

platforms. If you have concerns about the compatibility of your machine with the new Cricut Design Space plugin, simply check their system specifications page to see what is listed there for you and the operating system you are using.

HTTPS:/help.cricut.com/hc/en-us/articles/360009556033-System-Requirements-Design-Space-System-Requirements-Design-Space

Can I Use Design Space on My Chromebook?

Unfortunately, Cricut's Design Space is not currently configured for Chromebook operating system compatibility. This is because a current hurdle for that operating system is the need to import the plugin for the program, but this is not to suggest that in the near future, there is no hope for convergence.

Can I use the Design Space on more than one of my devices?

Yeah, all of your templates, elements, fonts, transactions, and images are available from any machine with an internet connection and your account credentials, thanks to Cricut's web-based and cloud-based features. This way, when you're out and about for the day, you can start a plan, then tie it up when you're back in your crafting space.

How many times can I use an image I buy in the Design Space?

Any design asset or element you buy from the design space is yours to use as many times as you like when you have a Cricut Design Space active account! Feel free to remove as many of the pictures as you can!

I accidentally welded two images. How do I unweld them?

Unfortunately, there is currently no dedicated option for unwelding available in Design Space. However, if you are welding an image, you can always press Undo if the improvements to your project have not been saved. At each separate point, it is advised that you store your photos locally, so you have clean images to work with on any project.

What types of images can I upload through Cricut's design space iOS or Android apps?

Any pictures saved on your Apple or Android machine in the Photos or Gallery app can be imported! If you have SVG files saved, they can also be imported.

Suppose you are attempting to upload. PDF or.TIFF files, it should be noted that they are not sponsored by Cricut Design Space.

What is an offline mode for Cricut Design Space?

This is a feature available on the iOS app only. Through this feature, you can download your items for use in an offline environment later. This is ideal if you plan on working on your designs in a space that does not have active internet access for an extended period of time. At the time, you can always focus on your tasks without dreaming about losing any fresh ideas!

What is available to download for offline use?

For offline usage, any feature or asset that you personally own or for which you have acquired rights through Cricut Design Space is available for download. This includes photos you have imported from other machines, images, or properties that you have gained from active membership in Cricut Access. It is up to you to select by hand what services you want to make available for offline use.

How do I save projects so I can use them offline?

Only with an active internet link will this move be completed, so make sure that you update before you go offline. Open a project that you want to save for offline use and pick the option "Save As." Pick the option "Save to this iPad/iPhone," and this will allow you to access this project without a connection at a later time.

How many images can I move to one mat?

The number of photos you can place on a mat is currently not limited. You're all clear if they suit!

Can I save money by hiding images from the mat?

The project price is not changed to indicate whether photographs have been obscured or not. If the picture has been used in some capacity in the design, the charge for that aspect would be incurred.

Can I save the layout of my mat?

Currently, mat templates will not be stored. The adjustments made to all your mats will be reset when you return to your canvas. Try taking a screenshot if you need to recall the style!

Is Cricut Design Space compatible with the current version of my internet browser?

Internet Explorer has started to be phased out by Microsoft. As such, the components of Cricut Design Space are not up to date or able to keep up with it. Check the Cricut website for the latest up-to-date device and browser specifications detail. The new versions of the following browsers are compliant with Cricut Design Space at the time of publishing, however.

- Apple Safari
- Google Chrome
- Microsoft Edge
- Mozilla Firefox

Take the time to familiarize yourself with it, get your bookmarks and favorites imported, and then visit design.cricut.com to download the plugin if you turn to one of these Internet Explorer browsers. Setting up your machine from here would be a breeze, and you'll be off and crafting in no time!

What are Features Available on Which Apps?

Here is a handy chart that lays out exactly what features are available in the Cricut Design Space, as well as what platforms support each feature! Be sure to consult this chart if you're weighing the options of which platform to get for your crafting experience.

Feature	Desktop Machine	iOS App	Android App
3D layer visualization		✔	
Attach	✔	✔	✔
Bluetooth compatible	✔	✔	✔
Contour	✔	✔	✔
Curve Text	✔		
Cut & write in one step	✔	✔	✔
Flatten to print	✔	✔	✔
Image upload	✔	✔	✔
Knife Blade cutting	✔		
Link Physical Cartridges	✔		
Machine setup	✔	✔	✔

ine		✓	
tern fills	✓		
to Canvas		✓	
it then cut	✓	✓	
e and weld	✓	✓	✓
art Guides		✓	✓
pchat		✓	
tem fonts	✓	✓	✓
nplates	✓		
ting style fonts	✓	✓	✓

How can I keep my Cricut mats sticky for longer?

You'll find a semi-rigid piece of transparent plastic stuck to the front of it when you purchase a new Cricut mat. You should place it back on top of your mat after each project if you save this piece of plastic, to ensure that nothing can stick to it between your tasks. This will prevent stuff from being stuck to and damaging the adhesion of your Cricut mat, like pet fur, glitter, paper scraps, and dust!

Is there anywhere else to get weeding tools?

Harbor Freight and other related hardware stores market hook sets that are equivalent to Cricut's weeding tool. In general, these collections of weeding hooks have a very low price point and do the job just as well as the patented weeding hooks of Cricut. If you think this is a tool you sometimes need to substitute, consider searching for a decent alternative on a budget and in bulk at Harbor Freight or another hardware store!

How should I weed my more intricate designs?

There is a method known as Reverse Weeding with more intricate designs. This is a technique that is mostly practiced on vinyl when the design introduces a design with a number of very thin or curly sections. If the vinyl has been run over, stick the transfer tape to the front of the pattern for some weeding.

To totally burnish the transfer tape down to the vinyl design, use your scraper. This will encourage it to stick to it so that when you get to the weeding process of this hack, nothing unnecessary pops up.

When you've done this, strip it all away from the contact surface, and remove the extra vinyl from the transfer tape using your weeding tool. This has been shown to remove a lot of tearing and stretching in projects like this that can happen.

Burnish it on your furniture piece as usual until all the waste is stripped from the design, and then cut the transfer tape exactly as you would normally.

My mats keep curling when they're stored. How should I store them?

It was discovered, by many artisans in the village, that the safest way to store the Cricut craft mats is to use wall space and command hooks. It stops them from sliding behind the furniture, losing themselves on the table in piles, or being hurt in the shuffle.

They're always kept straight and clean, and they're always right where you need them to be if you have them stuck up on the wall.

Do I have any alternatives when it comes to transfer tape?

One trick that a variety of craters, writers, and YouTubers swear by is purchasing and using contact paper at transfer tape from either Goal or the Dollar Tree! Nearly anywhere, contact paper is available, and you can get a lot of it for a very affordable price. The adhesive on contact paper is intended to be withdrawn with little or no residue after months or even years of use. This consistency makes it a perfect replacement for transfer tape, which we rely on to hold all our project parts between the carrier sheet and our project materials precisely in place!

How do I sharpen my Cricut's blades?

A very common Cricut trick in use is to stick your Cricut mat with a new, fresh piece of foil and run it through with the blade you are sharpening with. It helps to revitalize their edges and run the blades across the thin metal and give them a little more lasting strength before it's time to buy replacements.

Another way to do this is to make a foil ball, remove the blades from the housing, and several times insert them into the foil ball until you see a shine on the tip. This will give you a better understanding of how sharp the blades are when you finish them because it sounds like a more efficient way to sharpen several blades in one sitting, but the results appear to be about as positive as making the machine focus on one blade at a time for you.

My mat isn't quite as sticky as it used to be. How do I keep my projects in place?

You'll find that your mat will steadily loosen its hold on your ventures in certain areas as time goes on. To keep your designs in place, try using masking tape or painter's tape before giving up and tossing your pad away while it still has any of the traction left on it. When they're being sliced, this will keep the materials in place, but the glue is not heavy enough to ruin the project or mat, and it won't leave a stain.

It can be an invaluable advantage in your crafting to have a fresh mat with a firm grip, and it helps your projects run so smoothly. When you're trying to work, getting that hold on the mat is like having an additional pair of hands. The realists in the crafting world, however, realize that repairing your mats is not always practical as soon as they start losing their hold.

How can I adhere my designs to a rounded surface with no bubbles or wrinkles?

If you transfer a decal into something that is rounded, such as a cup or bowl, if you cut intermittent slits in the transfer film, you can find it much easier to lay the decal flat. Although this makes it difficult to reuse the piece of tape, you will find that this way, they will lay down much better on the floor.

How do you see your cut lines in the glitter iron-on material?

Because of the existence of glittery iron-on deflecting light in any way, it can be very hard to find your cut lines, and as a result, the weeding can require a touch of an extra tie. However, you can see the cut lines even more plainly if you use a small amount of baby powder and smooth it over the back of the design.

For this, you need just a very small quantity of powder, and you will find that the powder does not interact in any way with the design or its adhesion!

Is there an organized way to store my material scraps?

One of the many great things about organized citizens is that they love to teach other persons how to organize them! The internet culture Cricut has recently erupted with this hack. Keep a page protector binder and use such protectors as pockets for all your paper-size or smaller content scraps.

You can organize your scraps in whatever way you want for only a few bucks, hold them all intact, and never fear whether they have been wrinkled or broken to be used in your future ventures!

6.2. Cricut Hacks

1. Pegboard Tool Storage

At the end of the instrument, each patented Cricut instrument you have comes fitted with a very useful eyelet. This makes keeping their accessories by hanging them up really simple. In a crafts room, a pegboard makes it too amazingly easy to hang up your instruments in your crafting room.

You will get all your equipment arranged and set out right over your room right before your eyes. No more searching in drawers or bins, no more scuffing the instruments, no more worried about corners or chipping them.

The more open your instruments are, the better I find it to be to reach me for ideas for awesome projects!

2. IKEA Grocery Bag Holders as Material Organizers

For shopping bags that feature symmetrically arranged circular holes, IKEA offers very reasonably priced plastic dispensers. This makes them perfect for carrying one of several Cricut material rolls. They cost just $2.99 each, and you can keep all your rolls of material from folding, creasing, wrinkling, or even being harmed with one or two of them.

Plus, with how adorable all the materials are, they build on their own a pretty decent decoration product!

3. Use a Lint Roller

It might seem a little obvious after I clarify this one a little bit, but I guarantee it really is a lifesaver that will save you a lot of trouble as well as retain the gripping power on your mat. Small pieces of dust and dirt will make their way into your mat as you do more and more tasks. You will find a buildup of dust, dirt, and bits of paper, glitter, cloth, and more as they do. In order to maintain the hold on them, because Cricut firmly advises against cleaning the mats, it is imperative to practice due care to make them last.

This process has been sworn in by a substantial number of artisans and suggests that it has brought weeks to the lives of their Cricut mats. However, as Cricut does not support any efforts to strengthen the staying strength of the grip on their mats, it is better to hold off using this hack until you're confident you'd really like a new mat so that you can get a new one without feeling like you've missed something if it doesn't function well.

As Target will work just fine for this hack, lint rollers from the dollar store or the dollar section, so there's no need to break the bank to buy yourself a lint roller for this job, either!

4. Use Non-Alcohol Wipes to Clean your Mats

Since Cricut firmly urges your mats not to be washed, it is imperative that you know that you do this at your own risk. A decent number of individuals have tried this hack, though, and find it to be a perfect way to give a few extra weeks of life to their mats.

Since Cricut does not support any efforts to strengthen the staying strength of the grip on their mats, it is best to hold off using this hack until you're confident you'd really like a new mat so that you can get a new one without feeling like you've missed anything if it doesn't function well.

Using baby wipes or non-alcohol wipes on your mats can loosen stuff caught in your mat's grip, clean away dirt or paper leavings, which can give your mats a few more weeks of grip power!

5. Wash Your Mats with Soap, Water, and a Gentle Scrubber

Since Cricut firmly urges your mats not to be washed, it is imperative that you know that you do this at your own risk. A significant number of Cricut crafters, however, said that this little tip prevented them from at least having to purchase a new mat for an additional few weeks.

Since Cricut does not support any efforts to strengthen the staying strength of the grip on their mats, it is best to hold off using this hack until you're confident you'd really like a new mat so that you can get a new one without feeling like you've missed anything if it doesn't function well.

You should gently clean the adhesive grip side of your mat using warm water (do not go too hot; otherwise, you might melt the adhesive on your mat) and a gentle dish soap like Dawn, Fairy, or Palmolive, and the soft side of a kitchen sponge. As you don't want to grind debris more in, don't add too much pressure, or just scrape the adhesive entirely off the mat.

When you have done this, clean the mat well and pat dry with a linen dishtowel or a high-quality paper towel that will not leave any dirt behind. Set the pad to dry entirely for an hour or two after you have done this, and then give it a shot and see how much the wash has helped you out.

Over time, doing all these hacks will give you a sense of what works, what doesn't, and how much you just need to swap your mats with Cricut.

6. Clean your Blades

You may find that your blades are snagging on your products after some period of repeated use or that the cuts are not as crisp as you might light up for them to be. Take the house from its accessory clamp if you are struggling with this, then press the button at the top of the house. This will stretch the blade outside of the housing, so when you clean it, it will still allow you a firm grip on the blade.

If there is some gunk visible on the blade, pinch around the shaft of the blade and drawback, using a very deliberate grip between the opposite thumb and forefinger, making sure you do not go against the angle of the blade as you do. This should strip from the tip of your blade all foreign materials, making your cuts more effective.

You may also take a tin foil ball and stab the blade multiple times into the ball, which will remove debris when doing a light sharpening on them as well.

7. Leave the Material Dial on your Explore Set to Custom

One of the concerns that many consumers of Cricut Explore have is remembering to adjust the dial for the right content they have loaded into the machine at the top of their machine. If you do this, you might find that the stuff you've put into it is pressing your blade too hard or not hard enough.

Leaving the machine on the setting you last used is very normal, which can then create complications when you're doing the next one. As a solution to this problem, at the end of each job, many crafters find it a tradition to set their dial to "Custom," as you won't know what material you might use next for your Cricut.

Leaving the dial set to "Custom" would allow the Cricut program to ask you at the beginning of each project what sort of material is in the unit. Because of this dilemma, it removes the risk of ever cutting too many or too little.

8. Remind Yourself

If you don't think that the answer for you is to leave your machine on "Custom," or if you have trouble remembering to do that part, make yourself a craft project! Create a vinyl decal that reminds you to turn the dial and brush it on the side of your Cricut Explore unit at the beginning of your tasks!

Bonus Hack: Don't forget to cut slits in the edges of your transfer tape so you can go along the curved edges!

9. Test it out

Do yourself a favor and run a test if you're going to do a big job, a project with a lot of complicated cuts, or a project on a material you've never seen in the past.

On the settings that you would like to use, set your machine to cut only a basic form from the material to make sure your blades are sharp enough, the settings are tight enough, and that the material is right for your machine.

Using this would avoid waiting for the conclusion of a layout, only to discover out half the lines have not come out correctly. This is a waste of time, of commitment, of money, and of heartbreak!

10. Flip Your Canvas

There is a great large hollow spot in the middle for drawing canvases or canvas that is placed on a wooden frame. The wooden frame on which it is placed provides a large hollow spot that you can't put pressure on. It could be stretched by placing pressure on the spot on the canvas, thereby making the designs uneven, not sitting perfectly, or just wonky in general.

A change of approach would be required for the right way to get the concept burnished on a canvas. When you have the transfer tape layered with your template on your canvas, all appropriately placed as it is supposed to be, so you may want to give it a tentative one-over with the burnishing tool so that it sticks, then turn your canvas so that your design is face down on your work area.

You will burnish the back of the painting so that it is upside down. Offer it a detailed rub on the back of the canvas, in the middle of the wood frame, with your burnishing tool, and apply all the pressure you need to get your pattern to adhere to the bumpy texture of your canvas. This enables you, without losing the tautness of your canvas, to apply the energy.

You should turn it back over, cut the transfer tape, and enjoy your handiwork until your template is completely burnished! See the next hack in this segment if you need help for the transfer tape to come up from the canvas without the job of sticking to it.

11. Roll Your Transfer Tape

Perhaps, when you are attempting to delete it, you will find that a surface is more appropriate for making a pattern adhere to the transfer tape. By using the XL Scraper tool from Cricut, the best tip I've found for getting around this is. Peel the first corner of your pattern and put the XL Scraper right at the fold of the tape that you are cutting, round side up.

When you cut the tape, as it is being pulled up, begin to force the XL Scraper into the crease of the transfer tape. This will help allow the template letters and lines to remain placed on the surface while you remove the transfer tape!

In my experience, this hack is most effective for surfaces such as canvas, wood, or slate. You should reflect on the need to use this procedure to cut the transfer tape, whether there is a rough or porous surface. It's going to make your life much better.

12. Use Heat to Encourage Sticking

If you're using a porous substance like slate, wood, or cloth and your vinyl doesn't feel like it's going to stay where it should, pull out your heat gun or your trusty hairdryer!

You would not want to use a lot of heat on them because the materials for your Cricut are not really durable materials. What you want is to give them enough heat that the adhesive begins to grasp the surface crannies under your design. Melting the concept could affect the way it looks or hurt it dramatically, which is not what we want.

Try to keep the heat source flowing over your architecture in order to minimize the heat on your model. Keep the heat gun or hairdryer a fair distance from the surface, and do not concentrate the heat in any one location.

13. Go for the Straightener

If you have a decal that you have designed from iron-on vinyl, and you want to place that design on a special object, your best bet for adding heat to get the design to remain on your item could just be your hair straightener.

Your straightener can add heat to a small room, can be quickly maneuvered, and has less risk of burning or melting the plastic components of the object on which you want to iron your decal.

14. Use Parchment Paper Instead of Teflon Sheets

Before looking at Cricut as a craft, if you're like me and have never even heard of Teflon papers, you would be pleased to know that the parchment paper you can buy in bulk at the grocery store in the baking aisle can serve just fine.

This guide is used mainly as a barrier for the iron-on designs and the source of heat you are using. It helps avoid scorching and freezing, and the diffusion of heat is good for parchment paper.

However, take care when using this process, as placing too much heat on the paper for a prolonged period of time in one position may burn it or cause scorching.

This is one of those in-a-pinch tips that can get you to a few measures, but the easiest, simplest thing to use for iron-on decals is Teflon papers.

15. Put Water in That Glass

Put some water in it if you are going to put a decal on the outside of a vase, drinking glass, shot glass, pot, etc. It will be your level to remind you how high your design should be and will help you retain the level of all your design components.

Before you stick to the plan, make sure there is no liquid on the exterior of the bottle! You wouldn't like to have it destroyed.

16. Invert Your Pens

You can store the Cricut pens that you can place in Accessory Clamp A upside down. This will help you store all the ink in a pen at the tip, keep the tip from drying out, and provide you with clear, crisp lines anytime you use them, no matter how long it's been. Don't think about having to shake, soak, or uninstall your markers with this hack!

17. Branch out with your Markers

Some Cricut group members have said they have found other marker brands, particularly Crayola, to be excellent replacement markers for their Cricut method. In terms of color and design, you can get more variety without the prohibitive expense or choices that the Cricut brand has to sell. Try a range of numerous labels to see what fits for you!

18. Use Rubber Pen Grips

If you choose to use markers that are not the Cricut brand, you can find that the pens are not large enough to fit correctly into accessory clamp A. Get any of the rubber or silicone pencil grips that are not bent on the outside in such a case, and slip one around the marker. Using so will make it large enough to maximize your experience!

19. In a Pinch, Use a Hair Tie

If you notice that you have a pen that you want to use with clamp A, but you don't have a pencil grip on your palm, loop a hair tie a couple of times around the grip area and try it for fit!

To get the fit exactly right, you can need to try a few different times, but this will also do the trick of holding a non-Cricut pen in place in clamp A!

20. Pigeonhole Your Strong Grip Transfer Tape

The transfer tapes from Cricut are available with different grip strengths. The transfer tape for the Hard Grip really lives up to its tag. If the adhesive is too heavy when you're using transfer tape on your projects, it could stretch or ruin your design, and no one wants that.

However, this transfer tape is not without its applications. It is my suggestion that you exclusively use your good grip transfer tape on glitter-coated vinyl. The extra grip will allow the vinyl to adhere to the transfer tape while you work without destroying any portion of the design.

The shimmer provides a coarse surface to the surface of the vinyl that can make it hard for a tape to hang on to. This tape is going to hang onto the stuff, so your designs won't hurt. Other transfer tapes seem to have a hard time sticking to the glittery surface, but a match made in heaven seems to be the glitter vinyl and Cricut's Tight Grip Transfer Tape!

21. Weaken Your Transfer Tape

You may want to take a few minutes to soften it if you find yourself in a bind with a transfer tape that is better than what you need for the project you're doing. This is achieved very quickly by peeling away the transfer tape from the carrier layer or backing and adding the transfer tape to a fabric surface such as linen or your jeans. Anything that a lot of fibers won't leave behind, so that's going to degrade that adhesive.

22. Washi Setting for Intricate Designs

If you make a very complicated or fragile vinyl pattern, you can find that the blade is not as delicate as it needs to be for the job at hand. Using the 'Washi Tape' or 'Washi Board' setting for the cuts if this is the case. Washi tape and washi sheets are a very fragile substance, and this is expressed by the settings on your machine. This should send you some responsive outcomes that you're looking for. Don't hesitate to reverse your more critical designs with marijuana to keep intact the fine and nuanced lines!

23. Strong Grip Lint Roller

You can find that a lot of fabric debris and fibers get attached to the mat over time if you are a crafter who does a lot of projects with the pink mat, which is primarily designed to carry fabric. If this is the case, take some of the Good Grip Transfer Tape and put your pink mat on the sticky side.

To extract the fiber and dirt, do this many times over the whole surface of your pad. Since experimenting with felt, flannel, linen, burlap, and other fabrics that have loads of fibers, consider doing this. You can find that this will clear a lot of the unwelcome debris from your mat, leaving behind a good tat grip to continue doing your best job in your crafting!

24. Remove Bubbles in Your Vinyl Designs

Roll the rounded back of the scraper over the pattern to drive them toward the outside sides if you notice that you have bubbles on your vinyl. You can find that you need to use a fine blade for very stubborn air bubbles to pop the bubbles and smooth them down with your finger or scraping tool. In cases such as these, the rubber roller is also good support!

25. Give Your Transfer Tape a Good Rubdown

Return the transfer tape over the design and send it very detailed burnishing if you notice that a design has a lot of bubbles in it. Using it can help you sort out any air bubbles that have appeared without allowing the template to streak or scrape.

It's important to burnish very thoroughly and check for bubbles and wrinkles before removing the transfer tape in the first place. This is the best moment to burnish away without thinking about the design getting scuffed, so go nuts!

26. Remove Your Transfer Tape at an Angle

In your style, the easiest way to eliminate the risk of making bubbles or wrinkles is to peel off one corner of the transfer tape and remove it all by pulling it up or down at an angle. It could bring air between the template and the crafting surface by pulling straight up. You may also use your XL Scraper to hold your letters down while using this form, as illustrated in one of the tips above. When eliminating the transfer tape will help keep the letters on even ground while negative pressure is applied!

27. Iron-On Material Works Great with Wood

You may consider trying iron-on vinyl if working with wood is fascinating to you and you like making plaques and other beautiful wooden designs. When heat is applied, the thickness of the material and the solid hold it provides make it a perfect candidate for easily sticking to a porous surface.

With this procedure, make careful that the iron never comes into close contact with the wooden surface; otherwise, you can end up destroying the wood by moisture or scorching! If you need to, keep your Teflon sheets practical and iron on in bursts!

28. Don't Remove Your Design from the Mat before Weeding

On the mat, weed! This is a common term that my Cricut crafters, who are looking to help new crafters who are getting used to Cricut, can hear tossed your way. Before beginning the weeding process, the removal of the vinyl from the Cricut mat is a frequent mistake made by novice crafters. Weeding your template on the mat, though, makes it even simpler for you. Think of the grip as an additional pair of hands that holds the pattern where it wants to be when you're weeding. On the mat, weed!

29. Use a Lint Roller to Weed Your Cardstock

Weeding it will take a bit of extra time when you have a cardstock pattern on your mat that has just been cut. However, the cardstock waste will adhere to the lint roller if you use a lint roller. With practice, with all of your cardstock designs, this approach will cut your weeding time in half!

30. In a Pinch, Use a Fork

A fork can be an unexpected alternative if you find yourself in the midst of a project and you can't find your weeding tool or if your weeding tool has broken! This works mostly on vinyl, and toothpicks are another suitable alternative that you can find more effective! In your crafting, try a few other implements to see what works well for you!

31. Save Your Old Gift Card

Using an old or unused gift card is a perfect stand-in if you don't have your scraper or burnishing tool ready! For smoothing down corners, working out bubbles, scratching up trapped edges, working rises or crevices, the flat edges and narrow shape are very useful for everything the scraping tool is good for! Don't get me wrong, the scraping tool Cricut is worth its gold weight, and then some. For all its separate uses, it is an ideal method, but in a hurry, a gift card can get the job done with a bit more finesse and elbow grease!

32. Use Fabric Barrier for Your Iron-Ons

Using a Teflon sheet is common when ironing on a decal that you've made. It tends to diffuse and spread the heat equally, meaning there is no scorching on the decal from the iron. However, if you use normal cotton cloth and hold the iron going, this same result can be accomplished.

Please don't allow the iron to sit on the decal so that it might get so much heat into it. In case you don't have a Teflon sheet on hand for your craft, using this method will help you achieve your ironed result with little or no harm!

It can be a temporary measure to use a cotton fabric instead of Teflon before you know if iron-on is something you'll frequently deal with! Then you should spend the money on a Teflon sheet until you're committed to the art!

33. Pump up the Pressure

When your blades start losing their sharp edge, before sharpening or removing them, you should raise the pressure in your Cricut settings to get the most out of your blades! Before eliminating or repairing them, this is a perfect way to ensure that you use your blades to their maximum potential!

34. Add a Placeholder Shape in Design Space

You will find it is not as easy to line up the supplies on your mat until you have started gathering scraps of the materials from your projects. You could end up with some dreary types or some forms that just aren't the width you're used to getting on your mat. The only way to make sure that the new concept suits the piece you have is to line it up with your project in the corner of the mat you want to use.

Using the dimensions until you've got it on the mat to tell you how large the piece is. In Cricut Design Room, build a blank square that is approximately the size of the piece you have on your mat. The Room of Architecture has dimensions in it that can be easily tailored to what you need.

When you have the shape in the Design Room, just use it as a scale for your project to ensure that the materials available to you match what you have!

35. Heat Makes Vinyl Easier to Remove

If you had a vinyl decal added to a board, but it didn't turn out just the way you expected it to, don't worry. You can release the glue with a heat gun or a hairdryer so that you can erase the decal or reposition it.

Be warned that the method of removal cannot be as gentle on the decal, so don't depend on being able to add it again. But oh, weird stuff has happened, huh? Nothing is unlikely in the world of crafting!

36. You Can Reuse Transfer Tape

With the carrier layer or safe backing, whether you are diligent and store the transfer tape, you can reuse decent transfer tape up to seven times until the adhesive is no longer sturdy enough to hold your designs! After one use, tossing your transfer tape away will cost you a lot of money, and you'll just get bored of driving over and over again to the craft store! Find a transfer tape brand that you need, stock up, and take as long to get as you can through each bit!

This is the best tip for making the value of your money with a material that, as a Cricut crafter, you simply cannot do without!

37. Mind the Cap

Place the cap on the back of the pen so you don't drop it while your Cricut pen or any form of a pen is in use in accessory clamp A! It's better to wrangle any and every accessory you can, as you go, with crafting projects that require too many tiny, losable pieces!

38. Maintenance

After a while, you may notice some of your projects coming out in a condition that is less-than-crisp. In this section, I'll outline a troubleshooting and maintenance checklist you can utilize to bring your Cricut machine back into peak working condition!

1. Ensure your machine is on a stable footing.

This may sound pretty simple, but it will help your machine to make more accurate cuts every single time to ensure that it is on a level surface. In your designs, rocking the machine or wobbling may trigger erratic outcomes.

Make sure there is no debris trapped under your machine's feet that could cause instability before progressing to the next stage of troubleshooting!

2. Redo all Cable Connections

So your connections are in the best working order possible, undo all the cable connections, blast into the ports or use compressed air, and then safely plug it all back into the proper ports. This would help to ensure that all of the ties speak to each other as they should be!

3. Completely Dust and Clean Your Machine

Tiny Cricut is working hard for you! Return the favor by making sure the surfaces and crevices do not cause gunk, mud, grime, or dirt to build up. Around the mat input and on the rollers, the adhesive will build upon the machine, so make careful to work on those places!

Use it to blast any small bits and pieces of material or dust which might have formed up along the cutting strip, bar and rollers, and pad input, whether you have a can of compressed air. Q-Tips can also be a wonderful resource for the tiny rooms of your machine to be washed out; place the rubbing alcohol for more use!

4. Check Your Blade Housing

Within the housing for your knives, dirt and leavings from your materials will also build up! Open them and clean out any built-up materials that could hinder swiveling or motion.

5. Sharpen Your Blades

A very common Cricut trick in use is to stick your Cricut mat with a new, fresh piece of foil and run it through with the blade you are sharpening with. It helps to revitalize their edges and run the blades across the thin metal and give them a little more lasting strength before it's time to buy replacements.

Another way to do this is to make a foil ball, remove the blades from the housing, and several times insert them into the foil ball until you see a shine on the tip. This will give you a better understanding of how sharp the blades are when you finish them because it sounds like a more efficient way to sharpen several blades in one sitting, but the results appear to be about as positive as making the machine focus on one blade at a time for you.

Conclusion

Thank you for making it through to the end of Cricut for Beginners. Let's hope that it was helpful and able to give you all the tools you need to accomplish whatever your goals may be.

Seeking projects and resources that excite you and dive straight in is the next step! I would love to see my readers welcome the huge amount of possibilities for creation that lie ahead of them now.

There is really no end to the incredible stuff that you can do with the instruments that you have bought for this craft. They're so flexible that the sky is the limit, with the imaginative strength applied to the flexibility.

Finally, a recommendation is always welcomed if you find this book beneficial in some way.

CPSIA information can be obtained
at www.ICGtesting.com
Printed in the USA
BVHW070302280421
605953BV00001B/17